Good for the USA
Buyer's Guide 2017

Helping Americans choose the global products
that support American jobs.

Thomas J Johnson

Good for the USA Buyer's Guide
2873 Ocean Avenue
Seaford, New York 11783
www.GoodfortheUSA.com

@GoodfortheUSA

admin@goodfortheusa.com

Ordering Information:
Quantity sales. Special discounts are available on quantity purchases by corporations, associations, and others. For details, contact the copyright owner at the address above.

ISBN: 1542544785
ISBN-13: 978-1542544788

PREFACE

The origin of the *Good for the USA* rating system dates back to 2004 when the author personally saw American jobs being lost at his business contacts. At the time, publishers were not interested and self-publishing was not a viable option. So, the author used the rating system for his personal and business buying until 2016 when job losses became an issue in the Presidential campaign. With more publishing options, *Good for the USA Buyer's Guide 2017* is now available for all Americans.

CONTENTS

CHAPTER ONE

HOW DOES THIS BOOK WORK?

It's actually a very simple concept. American companies are sending jobs overseas. They are manufacturing products in other countries and shipping those products back to the United States for sale to the American people. They're doing this to reduce labor costs, avoid U.S. environmental laws and make more profit. Complaining to the companies doesn't change things and politicians can only do so much while the American manufacturing base and; therefore, the American tax base, is disappearing.

Groups have tried to organize "Buy American" campaigns, but you can tell they aren't working by the frequent news stories about closing factories. An effective "Buy American" effort simply takes too much time and costs too much money for most Americans.

This book offers an easy alternative. Companies and their brands are ranked based on their *Good for the USA* rating.

The rating is based on the belief that if a company gets 50% of its global sales from the United States, it should have 50% of its employees in the United States. The brands that come closest to this ideal get the best rating.

To use the ratings, you shop for the product you want and compare the ratings for the brands you are considering. For example, if you are looking for a car, but you simply don't like any American cars, you can still aid American workers. If you've narrowed your search to a Honda, a Kia or an Audi, check their *Good for the USA* ratings. Honda earned 34 *Good for the USA* points with about 29,500 U.S.-based employees to Kia's 22 points with about 3,000 U.S. employees and Audi's -4 points with nearly no U.S.-based employees.

Clearly, in this example, a Honda purchase will support the most U.S. workers and contribute the most to the U.S. economy.

And, perhaps, most important, you can stay within your budget while supporting American jobs.

The rating is determined by five factors:

1) **U.S. Headquarters** **20 points**

2) **U.S. Employees vs. U.S. Sales Ratio**

3) **Bonus Points for Total Amount of U.S. Employees**

4) **No U.S. Manufacturing** **-20 points**

5) **No Foreign Manufacturing** **+20 points**

The final rating reflects the economic value of the company to the United States. Many foreign companies outscore American based companies. This is because some U.S.-based companies are importers that generate 100% of their sales from the United States with all manufacturing overseas.

For a more detailed explanation of the *Good for the USA* rating system, turn to chapter eight on page 189.

If you agree with the *Good for the USA* rating system, you can move on to the ratings on page 61 and begin to become a better, more knowledgeable U.S. consumer. If you need more convincing—or would like to get more annoyed and frustrated by the realities of global business—read the following chapters.

Good for the USA

CHAPTER TWO

WHY IS THIS BOOK "GOOD FOR THE USA"?

"It's the economy, stupid." Those were the words of Bill Clinton when he ran for President in 1992. The nation was in a recession, and he wanted voters to think about it. He wanted them to bring thoughts of a poor economy and a difficult job market into the voting booth. And they did.

Today, it's still "the economy, stupid." The circumstances are not the same, but the future of the U.S. economy is clearly at stake. In 1992, the pressures on the economy were national. Today they are global. Our jobs are going overseas, and our dollars are fueling the exodus. Many believe the North American Free Trade Agreement (NAFTA) was the beginning of the drain on U.S. jobs. NAFTA was negotiated by President George H.W. Bush during his presidency and signed into law during the presidency of Bill Clinton.

Upon taking office in 1993, President Clinton began seeking support for NAFTA. Ross Perot, the third-party candidate for president in 1992 and 1996, spoke out strongly against the North American Free Trade Agreement. In 1993, he said we would hear a "giant sucking sound" as American jobs are pulled south to Mexico. Perot's anti-NAFTA message resonated with the American people and hurt President Clinton's prospect of getting swift congressional approval for the treaty. President Clinton knew he needed the support of the American people before he could expect the support of congress.

The "giant sucking sound" comment earned Perot a 66% favorable rating through most of 1993. Then, on November 9, 1993, he agreed to debate Vice President Al Gore on the merits of NAFTA. The debate was billed as the showdown between the will of big government and the down-home thoughts of an average American citizen. At the time, the Gore-Perot debate was the most watched show on cable television.

It didn't go well for Perot. Al Gore accused him of being against NAFTA for personal gain. He successfully labeled Ross Perot as a greedy billionaire trying to block global progress for personal business reasons. Perot quickly lost his average American citizen persona. Gore was fast with the facts and demonstrated an in-depth knowledge of the treaty and its expected ramifications. Perot was obviously caught off guard and ill-prepared. After the debate, Perot's favorable rating dropped to just 29%. With the American people now backing NAFTA, the agreement passed in Congress and was enacted in January, 1994.

Fast forward to 2017, and the result has been Free Trade agreements with dozens of nations and several regions throughout the world. Support for these agreements has been bi-partisan, with President Clinton, President George W Bush and President Obama all signing many deals. President Donald Trump has spoken strongly against the trade agreements in their current form. You'll find democrats and republicans in support of Free Trade and you'll find democrats and republicans against Free Trade in its present form. The nation's news media are filled with opinions and facts both in favor of and against the agreements. For every "expert" claiming Free Trade is good, there's an "expert" saying Free Trade is killing the U.S. economy. While the discussion rages, Free Trade continues to eat away at the U.S. job base.

Free Trade is here to stay. Jobs are going overseas. And American companies are transforming themselves into global companies without loyalty to their home country. The United States has become just another market to many American companies. In fact, most companies don't even report the United States as an individual market. They report sales for the North American market or even the Americas market (including all of North and South America) as Apple does in its 2016 10-k report. Interestingly, Apple does report "Greater China" and Japan as two individual segments separate from the rest of Asia.

It's important to note, this is not exclusive to Apple. Very few companies report the United States as an individual market, even if the U.S. represents most of their annual sales. The number of employees is reported either globally or in the same market segment method.

So, is the loss of American jobs the fault of the politicians or the fault of the companies? No, the fault is shared by everyone, including the American people who buy less-expensive foreign made goods instead of U.S. made items. We all do it. Most people don't even know where their refrigerator, washer, television or stereo was made. The decision to buy was based on features and price, not country of origin. Even the most steadfast "Buy American" proponents are having a hard time finding American made goods.

The transfer of jobs to other countries is simple economics. If you own a small company making chairs, you would have to compete with many other chair companies just to get your merchandise into the retail stores. You would compete on quality, design and price. In the 1970s you may have been able to demonstrate that your chairs were better made than foreign chairs. Today, many nations have skilled work forces and access to the same machines and materials that your workers use to make chairs. Better quality is not an easy claim today. The same goes for design. If you design the year's most attractive chair, you can bet someone else will have a similar chair on the market before you can count your profits. That leaves price.

"The United States work force is the most productive work force in the world." We've heard this claim for decades. Is it true? Does it really matter? If your workers can make a chair in two hours compared to six hours in China (or Korea or Brazil or India or . . .), you should be able to compete. Well, maybe not if you're paying high American wages compared to low China wages. The extra productivity simply can't overcome the low salaries in China or other countries. Tack on higher overhead costs and taxes, and your United States manufacturing facility may be in trouble.

One of the theories about Free Trade and the welcoming of

foreign made goods into the United States has been that countries paying low wages will eventually have to raise wages as their nation's economy grows. As the number of job seekers goes down, companies will have to compete with each other to attract the best workers. The anticipated result is higher wages and better benefits. This occurred in Japan and South Korea in the 1970s, 80s and 90s. A strong Japanese economy with plentiful job opportunities for its citizens is good for Japan and good for the world, including the United States. Today, Japanese companies are exporting jobs just as fast as American companies, thereby helping other nations to eventually achieve the success that Japan and the United States enjoy. The problem with this "eventually" theory is that China and India each have more than a billion people. It will take a long time for these countries to run out of eager low wage workers. The fear is that the United States will run out of jobs before China reaches a point of fair pay for employment.

Now, let's get back to your American chair manufacturing company. When you convince the buyer at a retail store to offer your chairs in their stores, you are half-way home. Now, you need consumers (that's you and me) to buy your chair. Think back to the last time you bought a chair (or any similar product). Did you think about where it was made? You were probably too busy trying to stay within your budget. And you probably bought the nicest chair you could afford. That's the American way. It always has been, and it always should be. Choice and the freedom to choose is what made this country so prosperous.

But what does this mean to your chair business. If your chairs don't sell due to a higher price than your foreign competition, you have three choices . . . lower your price and risk going out of business, sell your business and get your investment out before it's too late, or outsource part or all of your manufacturing to a low-wage/low-regulation nation. Of course, there are many variations to each of these choices, but to keep this example simple, we'll use just these three.

Hundreds of U.S. manufacturers have faced this decision. Some have simply lowered their price and succeeded. Others have altered their product or manufacturing process to reduce costs, and others have repositioned their products to target a new market niche. Still, others have failed or sold to a larger company or outsourced production. The end result is often fewer American jobs or lower-paying American jobs. Companies that were forced out of business did not actually export American jobs overseas, but an argument can be made that uncontrolled and often unfair overseas competition resulted in the loss of those American jobs. Companies that outsourced production may not have actually hired overseas employees, but they did reduce their American job offerings. The companies in foreign countries that they contracted with helped to increase jobs in the foreign country at the direct expense of American jobs.

So, who's at fault here? You can't always blame the company . . . that's business. We can't expect an entrepreneur to continue to operate a business in a way that has no hope of making a profit.

And you can't always blame the consumer . . . choice is good. After all, very few of us have unlimited budgets. And $100 saved by buying a different chair can be used to buy that lamp we need for the bedroom.

So, what can we do to help save American jobs without going broke? We can ask the government to rewrite the laws regarding importation of foreign goods, but that might cause prices for everything to go up. Or we can just sit back and hope things work themselves out.

Neither of these solutions can work.

That is why this book is "Good for the USA."

This book seeks to unite American consumers in an effort to save American jobs. Not by "Buying American", but by buying from companies that employ U.S. workers. Which is better for our nation's economy: an American-based company that imports all of its products from overseas or a foreign-based company that makes its products in the United States with American workers? This book doesn't ask consumers to spend more money just to help American workers. This book asks you to shop within your budget and compare several brands. Then, if price and quality are equal, chose the brand that employs the most U.S. workers in relation to their American sales.

It's that easy.

CHAPTER THREE

FREE TRADE IS GOOD FOR THE USA

In 2015, according to World Bank data, the United States represented nearly twenty-five percent of the world's gross domestic product (GDP). GDP is a measure of the total value of all services and goods produced within a country. Compare this with the fact that the United States population is less than 5% of the world's total population and it becomes clear that the United States is much more prosperous than the rest of the world. Throughout the twentieth century, the United States moved further and further ahead of the world in standard-of-living and citizen prosperity. We'll discuss the reasons for this impressive success later in this chapter, but now let's discuss the ramifications of unchecked growth.

A testament to this success is the huge number of people trying to come to the United States from virtually every other country in the world. You don't hear of many people trying to leave the United States. People come to the United States for the opportunity to improve the lives of their family. They usually love their home country, but economic opportunity is often not available to the average citizen. In the United States, opportunity is available to every person. It seems that the only people saying they want to leave the United States are the people who have taken the greatest advantage of that opportunity—a few Hollywood actors. Of course, they will always come back to the USA to accept the millions of dollars they can make here.

As the United States moved ahead of the rest of the world and readily available news reports made it clear to people from less successful countries that Americans lived at higher standards, the people from those countries understandably wondered why they couldn't live like Americans. Many sought to come to America. Others accepted their position in life and still others sought to change their own governments or to blame the United States for all their troubles. In many cases this difference in wealth has led to hatred for the United States. While the causes for this hatred are very complex, this book chooses to look at the end result . . . the United States is loved and hated throughout the world. Hatred begins with governments of countries that feel they can't match the success of the United States. Instead of reforming their governments to allow the opportunities that are available to average Americans, these governments attempt to convince their people that the United States is evil. Reforming would put their stranglehold on power at risk, while demonizing the United States will solidify their power. As the United States grew in financial power and these countries stagnated, hatred for the United States strengthened.

It has become clear that an ever-widening gap between rich and poor countries will lead to trouble. That trouble can manifest itself in the form of a rush across the Mexican border, a growth in radical Islam, or many more hidden problems such as a huge transfer of technology to China through an extensive spy network.

The United States has been faced with a choice; isolate itself from the troubles of the world or help to improve the conditions in poor countries throughout the world. With more than seven billion people on earth and more than five billion of them living on less than $10 per day and nearly a billion in extreme poverty, it's clear the United States cannot invite them all to live and prosper in our country. Keep in mind, the United Nations uses $1.90 a day as the extreme poverty level. They conclude more than two billion people live on less than $3.10 per day. It's clear that the people the U.N. says are living above the poverty line includes many people that would be considered painfully poor by most Americans.

The United States cannot feed and clothe every poor person on earth. Even our vast relative wealth couldn't support two billion people. The many Free Trade Agreements seek to bring new economic activities to poor nations. They function as a way to spread the success of the United States without simply giving away money. They also attempt to escape the possibility of a future world where the United States and the developed world is too far ahead of the world economically to sustain itself. The idealistic goal of Free Trade is to bring the economies of poorer nations up while maintaining the high standard-of-living in the United States. If successful, the rush across the Mexican border would diminish because high paying jobs would be available in Mexico and South American countries. Radical Islamic leaders would have a harder time recruiting terrorists if living standards were acceptable to the people and China would be able to support its huge population without stealing American technology secrets.

The short-term reality is hardship for many Americans when family members lose jobs to overseas workers. Factories have closed and devastated the economies of countless American towns. But if open markets throughout the world work as planned, the future is bright for Americans and the entire world. The belief is that the American economy will reshape itself and continue to grow and produce high paying jobs.

This will happen only if Free Trade is fair to all participating countries. During the first twenty years of meaningful Free Trade, the United States is paying the greatest price. The Free Trade believers say this will change in the coming years as the gap between rich and poor nations diminishes.

When we look at that gap between our living standards and the rest of the world, we gain new appreciation for our lives in the United States. Talk to friends who grew up in other countries. Most often, you'll hear strong praise for the United States. Understandably, they will express pride in their homeland, but if you listen closely and ask about the differences between the lives of the average citizens of the United States and their country, you'll get the big picture. We all see television images of wonderful lifestyles in other countries. We see China undergoing tremendous growth in its cities. We see impressive homes in many other countries. But the reality is; the average citizen in China, and most other countries, lives in poverty. If you consider yourself an average American, you would probably have been an average Chinese citizen if you were born in that country. Be thankful you are in the United States where average is quite good.

Why is being average so much better in the United States than in most other countries? Some say it's because of the wealth of natural resources that early Americans found on the North American continent. Others say it's because of the bright and enterprising people who settled in the United States from all over the world. Without abundant natural resources and enterprising people, success in America may not have flourished as it did, but the truth is, you can find these attributes in many countries throughout the world.

The United States succeeded because of the system of government. That's it. That's the reason. While other countries were living under dictators and power-hungry monarchs, the United States was entrusting its people with the power to determine the rules of society. That's also why so many bright people from other countries came to America. They wanted the opportunity to succeed, and they were willing to work hard to achieve success. They weren't given those opportunities in their homeland, and they knew they would find them in America. It worked so well that many other countries are now trying to duplicate the American system and, ultimately, the American success story. It won't be easy because the U.S. has developed over the past 240+ years. Countries like Afghanistan didn't even have a banking system in place until the 21st century. They will need to build their system of government and commerce one brick at a time. This won't happen overnight. The United States success story for most Americans developed over generations. You live better than your parents did and they lived better than your grandparents did. Today, many people think only in the short term. Building success takes consistent effort, one day at a time.

Long-term Free Trade, if managed properly, may actually achieve a better world for everyone. It may take several generations, but it took several generations for the United States to develop into a global powerhouse. Look at our own history, the Americans of 1880 didn't live much better than the Americans of 1820. The industrial revolution brought potential and opportunity to America, and the American form of government allowed it to happen. It's time for the dictators and closely controlled governments of the world to allow the same types of opportunity for their citizens. Over several generations, Free Trade may cause that to happen.

So, the argument in favor of Free Trade comes down to two statements:

1) Unchecked growth in the United States while the rest of the world stagnates will ultimately lead to the downfall of the United States. Ancient Rome grew well beyond the standards of the rest of the world and, eventually, collapsed. Is the United States doomed to repeat history?

2) Carefully managed Free Trade can teach the world the proven ways to economic success while strengthening governments that will not become a threat to civilization. In history, the formation of the United States proves this is possible. Can it be managed on a global level? Look at Brexit and the struggles faced by the European Union as it continues to reform the European nations.

CHAPTER FOUR

FREE TRADE IS BAD FOR THE USA

How is it possible to claim "Free Trade Is Good for the USA" and "Free Trade Is Bad for the USA" in the same book? Actually, it's quite easy. The theoretical potential for Free Trade is obvious. A world with equal opportunity for all would result in greater prosperity for all and fewer conflicts between nations. The form of democratic capitalism practiced in the United States has proven to be the most successful form of societal structure in the history of humankind. If the entire world followed the lead of the United States, it would be a great world. To achieve that, Free Trade must be allowed to evolve for many decades.

The promise of Free Trade may one day become reality. That reality may not arrive for twenty, fifty or one hundred years, but the Americans of the future might be better off than they would have been if Free Trade never happened. Of course, that doesn't help the millions of Americans affected by lost jobs today. In the short term, Free Trade is bad for the USA. Free Trade as it is today is not fair trade. And most of the unfair aspects of Free Trade are harming the United States. The previous chapter focused on the theory of Free Trade and why it is necessary. This chapter will focus on the reality of Free Trade as we are living it today.

The United States government manages dozens of websites dedicated to promoting trade with the world. American exporters can search these sites for information on the country or countries where they hope to export their products and services. The U.S. Department of Commerce operates a website at www.export.gov. This site offers a wealth of information and links to other government sites for even more information. A look at the basic information pages reveals some disturbing facts about export opportunities to the Free Trade countries around the world.

After a few hundred clicks, you might find your way to www.buyusa.gov, a site managed by the U.S. Commercial Service. The *Privacy Policy* link brings you back to www.export.gov, so obviously www.buyusa.gov is a U.S. Department of Commerce site. It might be interesting to determine how many sites the U.S. government operates and whether these sites were made by Americans.

We're told that Mexico is a major trading partner with the United States. The U.S Department of Commerce lists *Market Opportunities* on its *Mexico Country Commercial Guide* page (https://www.export.gov/article?id=Mexico-Market-Opportunities). The first Opportunity says little more than "abundant market opportunities exist for U.S. firms in Mexico." The second, and most descriptive opportunity for American

Companies in Mexico states . . .

> Mexico's geographic proximity to the United States has propelled the maquiladora industry with thousands of factories near the U.S.–Mexico border for export back into the United States. This gives U.S. firms the opportunity to sell equipment and supplies to these factories or to use Mexico as an alternative to Asian manufacturing because Mexico's labor rates are "competitive" with China.

First, you might ask, "What is the maquiladora industry?" In colonial Mexico, "maquila" was the fee charged by millers when they processed grain for customers. In post NAFTA Mexico, "maquiladora" has come to mean the act of importing components, assembling them and exporting them back to the United States.

Is that it Uncle Sam? Is this what Free Trade and NAFTA are all about? U.S. companies can sell components to companies in Mexico or they can take advantage of lower manufacturing costs and ship the goods back to the United States where Americans will buy them. Thousands of factories are near the U.S.–Mexico border. Does that mean thousands of factories have left the United States and the U.S. workforce to move just outside the southern border? Do these factories abide by the myriad of U.S. government regulations relating to environmental controls, workforce rules and many other costly manufacturing issues? Of course not.

In fact, the NAFTA agreement permits Mexican trucks to travel on American roads. They are subject to the same safety checks that American trucks encounter on the roads. But it's no surprise that

U.S. truck regulations are much more strict than Mexican regulations. At a minimum, this means U.S. truckers are at a disadvantage because they must invest more in their trucks to keep them road worthy. At worst, it means American lives are at risk whenever a Mexican delivery truck drives by.

Now, let's assume an American company has a product it wants to export to Mexico for purchase by Mexican citizens. The first blockade to shipping goods to Mexico is a value-added tax (VAT). The VAT tax is used by more than 140 countries throughout the world. It is a charge on all products within the country and is charged at every point where value is added to an item. It essentially replaces a sales tax in these countries. In Mexico, items shipped to all parts of Mexico incur a 16% value-added tax. There is also a 0.8% processing fee on all items that do not benefit from NAFTA preferential tariff treatment.

It's argued that the value-added tax is not an unfair trade practice because VAT is also charged on all products made and sold by companies in the country, but the reality may be quite different. Companies shipping goods into VAT countries often pay the tax on the value of the goods plus shipping costs and insurance costs. The complex rules most countries enforce regarding VAT offer many opportunities for domestic companies to benefit from a somewhat lower total charge on similar items. And, in most cases, when products are exported from VAT countries, the VAT charges are removed. This is to avoid burdening the companies with the VAT charge from their country of origin as well as the VAT charge from the destination.

When shipping to the United States—which does not collect a value-added tax—these imported products may have a price advantage over domestic products. Companies making products in the United States pay many layers of taxes during the manufacturing process. These costs must be added to the selling price of the item. Imported products may not carry an equal tax burden once the value-added tax is removed.

That's Free Trade into the United States and not so Free Trade exported from the United States. Almost all of our trading partners charge an import tax on goods coming from the United States or any other country. The following pages list the charges imposed on products imported into selected countries throughout the world. All information was found on United States Department of Commerce websites.

Many of the listings include "CIF + duty". CIF stands for Cost, Insurance and Freight. Duty includes payments such as tariffs and other customs fees.

Argentina

TAX: There is a 21 percent value-added tax and a 0.5 percent customs administration fee. Both are charged on CIF + duty. Some products may be subject to additional taxes.

Australia

TAX: There is a 10 percent goods and services tax applied on FOB + duty.

Austria

TAX: There is a value-added tax of 20 percent for most products. Some products, such as basic necessities and foodstuffs, qualify for a reduced rate of 10 percent. The tax is applied on CIF + duty.

Bangladesh

TAX: 15 percent value-added tax assessed on CIF + duty. Additional taxes are applied on luxury items.

Barbados

TAX: 17.5 percent value-added tax assessed on CIF + duty.

Belgium

TAX: There is a value-added tax of 21 percent for most products. Some products, such as basic necessities and foodstuffs, qualify for a reduced rate of 1–12 percent. The tax is applied on CIF + duty.

Benin

TAX: There is a 15–20 percent VAT, a 1 percent statistical tax, and a 1 percent community solidarity levy. Agricultural, industrial, agro-industrial, livestock breeding, and the fishing industry products may be subjected to additional taxes.

Bolivia

TAX: There is a 13 percent value-added tax. There is a 1.94 percent customs users fee.

Brazil

TAX: The duty rate in Brazil ranges from 0 percent to 35 percent. The average rate is approximately 23 percent.

Burkina Faso

TAX: There is a 15–20 percent VAT, a 1 percent statistical tax, and a 1 percent community solidarity levy. Agricultural, industrial, agro-industrial, livestock breeding, and the fishing industry products may be subjected to additional taxes.

Cambodia

TAX: There is a 10 percent value-added tax for most products.

Cameroon

TAX: There is an 19.25 percent value-added tax on CIF + duty.

Canada

TAX: There is a 5 percent goods and services tax assessed on the duty-paid value (FOB + import duty).

Chad

TAX: There is an 18 percent value-added tax on CIF + duty.

Chile

TAX: There is a value-added tax of 19 percent applied on CIF + duty.

China

TAX: There is a value-added tax of 17 percent for most items. Necessities, such as agricultural products and utilities, are taxed at 13 percent. Small businesses (annual production sales of less than RMB 1 million or annual wholesale or retail sales of less than RMB 1.8 million) are subject to VAT at the rate of 6 percent. Also, consumption tax (2–3 , Provincial Tax, Not Uniformly Applied).

Congo, Democratic Republic of

TAX: There is a 16 percent value-added tax on CIF + duty.

Congo, Republic of

TAX: There is an 18.7 percent value-added tax on CIF + duty.

Costa Rica

TAX: Most products are subject to a 14 percent sales tax applied on CIF + duty.

Cote D'Ivore

TAX: There is a 15–20 percent VAT, a 1 percent statistical tax, and a 1 percent community solidarity levy. Agricultural, industrial, agro-industrial, livestock breeding, and the fishing industry products may be subjected to additional taxes.

Cyprus

TAX: In most cases, VAT is 15 percent. There is a reduced rate of VAT of 5 percent that refers mainly to food and agricultural products. VAT is charged on assets and services in Cyprus as well as on imports into Cyprus.

Czech Republic

TAX: The standard VAT rate is 19 percent and applies to most goods and services; a reduced rate of 5 percent applies to certain services and essential goods.

Denmark

TAX: There is a value-added tax of 25 percent for most products. Some products, such as basic necessities and foodstuffs, qualify for a reduced rate of 0 percent. The tax is applied on CIF + duty.

Dominican Republic

TAX: There is a value-added tax of 18 percent applied on CIF + duty. There is also a two percent surcharge. There is an additional tax on alcohol, soft drinks, matches, cigarettes, cigars, perfumes, jewelry, and carpets.

Ecuador

TAX: Most products are subject to a 12 percent tax applied on CIF + duty.

El Salvador

TAX: There is a value-added tax of 13 percent applied on CIF + duty.

Estonia

TAX: The standard VAT rate in Estonia is 18 percent. There are reduced rates of 0 percent and 5 percent.

Finland

TAX: There is a value-added tax of 24 percent for most products. Some products, such as basic necessities and foodstuffs, qualify for a reduced rate of 8–17 percent. The tax is applied on CIF + duty.

France

TAX: There is a value-added tax of 20 percent for most products. Some products, such as basic necessities and foodstuffs, qualify for a reduced rate of 2.1–5.5 percent. The tax is applied on CIF + duty.

Germany

TAX: There is a value-added tax of 19 percent for most products. Some products, such as basic necessities and foodstuffs, qualify for a reduced rate of 7 percent. The tax is applied on CIF + duty.

Ghana

TAX: There is a 15 percent value-added tax on most products applied on CIF + duty. There are additional taxes on some products.

Greece

TAX: There is a value-added tax of 24 percent for most products. Some products, such as basic necessities and foodstuffs, qualify for a reduced rate of 4–8 percent. The tax is applied on CIF + duty.

Guatemala

TAX: There is a value-added tax of 12 percent applied on CIF + duty.

Guinea Bissau

TAX: There is a 15–20 percent VAT, a 1 percent statistical tax, and a 1 percent community solidarity levy. Agricultural, industrial, agro-industrial, livestock breeding, and the fishing industry products may be subjected to additional taxes.

Honduras

TAX: There is a value-added tax of 12 percent applied on CIF + duty. There is also a 0.5 percent service charge applied on all items except for raw material and some capital goods. There is also a 20–50 percent excise tax applied to alcohol and cigarettes.

Hong Kong

TAX: Taxes are assessed only on automobiles, gasoline, tobacco, and alcohol.

Hungary

TAX: In most cases, value-added tax is payable at a rate of 27 percent. There is a reduced rate of 18 percent that relates mainly to some products and services.

Iceland

TAX: There is a value-added tax of 24 percent on most products applied on CIF + duty. There are additional taxes on some products.

India

TAX: There is a value-added tax of 5.5 percent on most products applied on CIF + duty.

Indonesia

TAX: There is a value-added tax of 10 percent applied on the CIF + duty. There is an additional sales tax on some luxury items.

Ireland

TAX: There is a value-added tax of 23 percent for most products. Some products, such as basic necessities and foodstuffs, qualify for a reduced rate of 4.8–13.5 percent. The tax is applied on CIF + duty.

Israel

TAX: There is a value-added tax of 17 percent applied on CIF + duty. Additional taxes may apply on some products.

Italy

TAX: There is a value-added tax of 22 percent for most products. Some products, such as basic necessities and foodstuffs, qualify for a reduced rate of 4–10 percent. The tax is applied on CIF + duty.

Japan

TAX: There is an 8 percent consumption tax applied on CIF + duty.

Jordan

TAX: There is a value-added tax of 16 percent applied on CIF + duty.

Kenya

TAX: There is a 16 percent value-added tax applied on FOB + duty.

Kuwait

TAX: There are no taxes on products shipped to Kuwait.

Laos

TAX: There is a 10 percent tax applied on CIF + duty. Some products are subject to additional taxes.

Latvia

TAX: The standard rate of VAT in Latvia is 21 percent. There are reduced rates of 0–9 percent.

Lebanon

TAX: There is a 10 percent value-added tax on CIF + duty.

Lithuania

TAX: In most cases, VAT in Lithuania is 21 percent; there is a reduced rate of 9 percent that applies to heating services. VAT on transport services in Lithuania is 5 percent.

Luxembourg

TAX: There is a value-added tax of 17 percent for most products. Some products, such as basic necessities and foodstuffs, qualify for a reduced rate of 3–12 percent. The tax is applied on CIF + duty.

Madagascar

TAX: There is a value-added tax of 20 percent applied on CIF + duty. There may be additional import taxes applied as well.

Mali

TAX: There is a 15–20 percent VAT, a 1 percent statistical tax, and a 1 percent community solidarity levy. Agricultural, industrial, agro-industrial, livestock breeding, and the fishing industry products may be subjected to additional taxes.

Malaysia

TAX: Sales tax varies by product: 5, 10 or 15 percent with 10 percent being the most common. It is applied on CIF + duty.

Mauritius

TAX: There is a value-added tax of 15 percent for most products.

Mexico

TAX: There is a 16 percent value-added tax assessed to most products. In addition, there is a 0.8 percent customs processing fee for products that do not qualify for NAFTA preferential tariff treatment.

Mongolia

TAX: There is a 10 percent value-added tax applied on CIF + duty.

Morocco

TAX: There is a value-added tax that varies between 0 and 20 percent depending on the product.

Mozambique

TAX: There is a 17 percent tax on all products. There is also a customs processing fee of $50 USD.

Netherlands

TAX: There is a value-added tax of 21 percent for most products. Some products, such as basic necessities and foodstuffs, qualify for a reduced rate of 0–6 percent. The tax is applied on CIF + duty.

New Zealand

TAX: There is a 15 percent goods and services tax applied on FOB + duty.

Nicaragua

TAX: There is a 15 percent value-added tax applied on CIF + duty.

Niger

TAX: There is a 15–20 percent VAT, a 1 percent statistical tax, and a 1 percent community solidarity levy. Agricultural, industrial, agro-industrial, livestock breeding, and the fishing industry products may be subjected to additional taxes.

Norway

TAX: There is a 25 percent value-added tax on most products applied on CIF + duty. There is a reduced rate of 12 percent on certain products, often basic necessities and food stuffs.

Oman

TAX: There are no taxes for products shipped to Oman.

Pakistan

TAX: There is a 17 percent sales tax applied on CIF + duty. Additional taxes may apply.

Papua New Guinea

TAX: There is a 10 percent value-added tax applied on CIF + duty.

Paraguay

TAX: There is a 10 percent value-added tax applied on CIF + duty. Some consumer products are subject to an additional 7 percent tax.

Peru

TAX: There is an 18 percent value-added tax applied on CIF + duty.

Philippines

TAX: There is a 12 percent value-added tax applied on CIF + duty.

Poland

TAX: In most cases, value-added tax is payable at a rate of 22 percent. There is a reduced rate of 7 percent that relates among other matters to sales of building materials, agricultural inputs, medications, musical instruments, baby products and more.

Portugal

TAX: There is a value-added tax of 23 percent for most products. Some products, such as basic necessities and foodstuffs, qualify for a reduced rate of 5–12 percent. The tax is applied on CIF + duty.

Qatar

TAX: There are no taxes for products going to Qatar.

Rwanda

TAX: There is an 18 percent value-added tax on virtually all goods with the exception of most products in Chapter 49 of the tariff schedule.

Saudi Arabia

TAX: There are no taxes for products going to Saudi Arabia.

Senegal

TAX: There is a 15–20 percent VAT, a 1 percent statistical tax, and a 1 percent community solidarity levy. Agricultural, industrial, agro-industrial, livestock breeding, and the fishing industry products may be subjected to additional taxes.

Singapore

TAX: There is a 7 percent sales tax on CIF + duty.

South Africa and the South African Customs Union (SACU)

TAX: Botswana and Lesotho have value-added taxes of 10 percent applied on the CIF + duty value.

Namibia currently has a value-added tax of 8 percent that is applied on the CIF + duty value.

South Africa has a value-added tax of 14 percent that is applied on FOB + duty value.

Swaziland may have a surcharge (amount unknown) levied on the CIF + duty value.

South Korea

TAX: There is a value-added tax of 10 percent applied on the CIF + duty value.

Slovakia

TAX: In most cases, VAT in Slovakia is 19 percent. There is reduced rate of 10 percent that applies in the main to food, medicines, fuel products and a large group of services.

Slovenia

TAX: The standard rate of VAT in Slovenia is 20 percent. There is a reduced rate of 8.5 percent for some products and services.

Spain

TAX: There is a value-added tax of 21 percent for most products. Some products, such as basic necessities and foodstuffs, qualify for a reduced rate of 4–7 percent. The tax is applied on CIF + duty.

Sweden

TAX: There is a value-added tax of 25 percent for most products. Some products, such as basic necessities and foodstuffs, qualify for a reduced rate of 6–12 percent. The tax is applied on CIF + duty.

Switzerland

TAX: There is an 8 percent value-added tax for most products. There is a reduced rate of 2.4 percent on certain products, often basic necessities and food stuffs.

Taiwan (Chinese Taipei)

TAX: There is a value-added tax (VAT) of 5 percent applied on the CIF value. There is also a port charge of 0.5 percent applied on the total CIF+duty+VAT for shipments by sea.

Thailand

TAX: There is a 10 percent value-added tax that is applied on CIF + duty.

Togo

TAX: There is a 15–20 percent VAT, a 1 percent statistical tax, and a 1 percent community solidarity levy. Agricultural, industrial, agro-industrial, livestock breeding, and the fishing industry products may be subjected to additional taxes.

Turkey

TAX: For most goods, there is an 18 percent value-added tax applied on CIF + duty. For basic necessities and foodstuffs, the rate is 8 percent. For electronics and some luxury items the rate is 26 percent.

United Arab Emirates

TAX: There are no taxes for products going to the United Arab Emirates.

United Kingdom

TAX: There is a value-added tax of 20 percent for most products. Some products, such as basic necessities and foodstuffs, qualify for a reduced rate of 0–5 percent. The tax is applied on CIF + duty.

Vietnam

TAX: There is a value-added tax between 10 and 20 percent applied on CIF + duty.

Venezuela

TAX: There is a 12 percent value-added tax for most products applied on CIF + duty. There is an additional 11 percent tax for some luxury items. 1 percent Customs Handling Charge applied on FOB for all imports.

Zimbabwe

TAX: There is a 15 percent value-added tax for most products applied on CIF + duty. There is an additional 10 percent surcharge on many products as well.

This list includes many of the world's countries or territories. Only a few do not charge an import tax. Interestingly, most of the tax-free nations are Arab countries; United Arab Emirates, Saudi Arabia, Qatar, Oman, Kuwait, and Bahrain. The others are Brunei and Bermuda. The United States is the only Western nation to allow vat-tax free importation.

The rest of the countries on the list tax imports at rates from 5% to over 20%. This tax rate listing was calculated based on the highest tax rate charged. Many countries have a variable rate system. After the taxes are paid, the tariffs come into play. Tariffs are extremely complicated. Each country has an ever-changing list of tariffs with different rates for different products. Historically, tariffs have been used to protect domestic manufacturers by pricing imports out of the market. The Free Trade agreements that the United States has signed over the past years seek to reduce tariffs.

If you want to spend countless hours researching tariffs visit www.export.gov. You'll find links to tariff information for nearly every country in the world. At the end of your research, you'll most likely be totally confused. Is this Free Trade tariff system Good for the USA or Bad for the USA? Some experts say "Good" and some say "Bad."

Let's just look at the facts.

According to the United States Census Bureau, the trade deficit was $745.66 billion in 2015. The trade deficit is determined by adding the value of all items exported from the United States to other countries and subtracting the value of all items imported from other countries. The result is a deficit for the United States. The United States has not experienced a trade surplus since 1975. For many other countries, the result is a surplus. The 2015 deficit means we received items that are consumed or depreciate in value (leaving us with very little), while our free-trading partners are left with $745.66 billion of our money. That's $745.66 billion removed from circulation in our economy.

In 2015, the United States imported $2.2 trillion worth of goods, while it exported $1.5 trillion worth of goods and services. Keep in mind, those components that we ship to factories across the border in Mexico count as exports, while the products they ship back to the United States count as imports. One result of Free Trade is that components that are made in America and consumed in America can become both exports and imports when shipped across the border for assembly.

The 2015 trade deficit with China was $367.2 billion. That's a bit less than fifty percent of the total 2015 trade deficit. What will

China do with that $367.2 billion? A recent spy incident caught the Chinese trying to illegally buy classified technology. They are also buying military weapons from Russia and other countries. $367.2 billion goes a long way towards building a world class military. An occasional read of your daily newspaper will reveal frequent reports on Chinese military advancements and demonstrations of Chinese military power.

The United States ended 2015 showing a trade deficit with all of our major trading partners including Japan ($68.9 billion), the European Union ($155.6 billion), Canada ($15.5 billion) and Mexico ($60.7 billion). If high deficits continue unchecked, it can't end well for the United States.

In 2015, the United States exported $2 billion worth of cars to Japan, but imported twenty-five times that amount ($50 billion) from Japan. Approximately 82% of Mexico's automobile exports went to the United States. Overall, we exported $55.3 billion in cars to the world while importing $169.1 billion. Compare this to other major car exporting countries and you'll see that, once again, the United States is alone in having a trade deficit.

2015 Automobile Exports and Imports in Billions of U.S. Dollars:

Country	Exports	Imports	Difference
United States	$55.3	$169.1	**deficit** $113.8
Canada	$44.96	$26.3	**surplus** $21.34
Germany	$152.7	$45.5	**surplus** $110.2
Japan	$86.1	$9	**surplus** $77.1
Mexico	$32.8	$9.5	**surplus** $23.3

For years, American news media have been reporting on the constantly growing trade deficit and what it means to our future. When Bill Clinton ran for President in 1992, he frequently mentioned the trade deficit as a problem that he would tackle if elected. After the election, he rarely mentioned the deficit during his eight years in office. In 1992, the United States trade deficit was at $84 billion. In 2000, the last year of Bill Clinton's administration, the trade deficit was $375 billion.

It has since grown to $745.66 billion with no end in sight. President George W. Bush saw the deficit more than double in his eight-year presidency. President Barack Obama saw the deficit drop during the depths of the recession in his first term and move back towards record levels in his second term. Like Bill Clinton, Bush and Obama didn't seem too concerned about it. Trade deficits seem to be major concerns during election season and simply not important thereafter. Democrats and Republicans appear to agree that the trade deficit should be left to grow larger and larger. What can an average, concerned American do if the elected government refuses to act?

You can start by writing to your representatives on the local, state and federal levels. Tell them you are concerned about the future stability of the United States. Ask them if they think it is wise to close our factories and put the manufacturing of important equipment in the hands of the Chinese Communist government. Ask them if they think it is wise to allow the Chinese Communist government to hold the bonds that finance our national debt.

After you've dropped your letter in the mail or pressed send, turn to the back of this book and start managing your purchases to buy from companies that are Good for the USA. Tell the world's companies that they can't take America for granted any more. Tell them that you bought their product because they employ American workers. Tell them that you didn't buy their product because they don't employ enough American workers. If enough concerned Americans contact enough companies, things just might change. These giant companies realize where the bulk of their sales come from. If they think they can cut American workers and still earn huge profits from the United States, they'll keep cutting workers year after year. If they think they can increase American sales by hiring more American workers, they might actually build new plants in the United States.

CHAPTER FIVE

A FEW WORDS ABOUT CHINA

More than sixty years ago, the United States fought a war in Korea. Speaking to his secretary of state, Dean Acheson, President Harry S. Truman said, "We've got to stop the sons of bitches, no matter what, and that's all there is to it." He was referring to the spread of communism.

After World War II, the Korean peninsula was split in two. The North was placed under the influence of the communist Soviet Union and the South was placed under western influence. In November, 1950, North Korean troops invaded South Korea. The North Korean army was heavily supported by the one-year-old communist regime from China.

More than 33,000 U.S. soldiers were killed during the three-year war. The Chinese and North Koreans lost hundreds of thousands. The war ended in 1953 when it was agreed that North and South

Korea would continue as separate nations. The spread of communism was stalled, but China and the Soviet Union were left to continue their communist control over the north.

More than fifty years ago, the United States fought a war in Vietnam. During a news conference on April 7, 1954, President Dwight D. Eisenhower referenced the domino theory and said. "Asia, after all, has already lost some 450 million of its peoples to the communist dictatorship, and we simply can't afford greater losses." The domino theory referred to one nation after another falling into communist control. "You have a row of dominoes set up, you knock over the first one, and what will happen to the last one is the certainty that it will go over very quickly. So, you could have a beginning of a disintegration that would have the most profound influences," said Eisenhower. This belief that American Presidents must impede the spread of communism continued from administration to administration.

The John F. Kennedy administration sent more than 11,000 military "advisors" to Vietnam. President Lyndon Johnson greatly increased involvement until more than 500,000 U.S. troops were fighting in Vietnam. From 1965 (the year Johnson's troop buildup began in earnest) through the end of the war in 1975, The United States lost more than 58,000 soldiers in Vietnam. The North Vietnamese and their allies lost millions of people in the war. In this case, communism was not stopped. Today, Vietnam is a communist nation.

More than thirty years ago, the United States was in the middle of the Cold War. The Soviet Union fought with the United States and the Allied forces to defeat Nazi Germany in World War II. The communist nation was rewarded for its contributions with the right to exercise influence over several areas of the world, including half of defeated Germany. East Germany remained a communist nation until the Soviet Union was dismantled in the late 1980s.

The decades leading up to the end of the Soviet Union were filled with fears and tense moments. The Soviet Union was determined to spread its communist beliefs throughout the world. The United States and other western democracies sought to stop the Soviet Union wherever possible. While a major war with the Soviet Union was always just around the corner, shots were never fired. This was the Cold War.

In a 1983 speech in Orlando, Florida, President Ronald Reagan warned the *National Association of Evangelicals* not to trust the Soviet Union:

> . . . be aware that, while [Soviet leaders] preach the supremacy of the state, declare its omnipotence over individual man, and predict its eventual domination of all peoples on the earth, they are the focus of evil in the modern world.

> . . . beware the temptation of pride—the temptation of blithely declaring yourselves above it all and label both sides equally at fault, to ignore the facts of history and the aggressive impulses of an evil empire, to simply call the arms race a giant misunderstanding and thereby remove yourself from the struggle between right and wrong and good and evil.

Like Presidents before him, Ronald Reagan saw the defeat of communism as an important American agenda. He greatly increased the U.S. military and watched as the Soviet Union tried to keep up. In the late 1980s, the Soviet Union was bankrupt. Many believe Ronald Reagan's arms race led directly to that bankruptcy and the end of the Soviet Union. Others believe the Soviet Union would have imploded without help from President Reagan.

Nearly fifty years ago, Fidel Castro seized power in Cuba and formed a communist government within ninety miles of the U.S. coastline. In 1959, Fidel Castro and his "26ᵗʰ of July Movement" overthrew the government of Fulgencio Batista. In the first few years of his dictatorship, Castro chose the communist form of government as best for his Cuba.

While he initially promised free and fair elections, within two years of taking power, Castro and Cuba quickly became a pawn in the Cold War struggle between Soviet Union Communism and the United States. Every President of the United States since President Eisenhower imposed economic sanctions on Cuba and sought to undermine and end Castro's power.

While the Soviet Union does not exist today, Cuba is still the only communist nation in the Western Hemisphere. In fact, Cuba is only one of four remaining communist nations in the world. North Korea, Vietnam and China are the other communist nations still in power.

It is quite clear that over the last sixty years, the United States has invested huge sums of money and tens of thousands of lives in the effort to stop communism. It is also clear that communist countries have invested heavily in their effort to harm the United States. Communist governments, like all totalitarian governments, have very different views relative to ruling their citizens. A

Chinese official once commented that America worries about losing one soldier on the battlefield while China can spare one million soldiers in a war effort without concern. The Chinese have also boasted about their ability to destroy west coast U.S. cities with their nuclear missiles.

Generations of Americans were raised with the understanding that communist nations are our enemies.

Why, then, is the United States government investing so much in the build-up of modern day communist China?

President Bill Clinton started the policy of helping China grow and Presidents George W. Bush and Barack Obama have expanded that policy. Most of their assistance is in the form of inaction to defend the American economy. China is our largest trading partner. China is benefiting from hundreds of billions of U.S. dollars. The communist Chinese government is spending our money on expansion in China and in purchasing global infrastructure.

China also engages the United States in global challenges year after year. In 2006, China announced a deal with Cuba that would allow them to drill for oil off the coast of Cuba in the Florida straits. United States oil companies are not permitted to drill in these waters for environmental reasons. China and Cuba do not abide by our environmental laws. This is just one example of China flexing its muscles at the United States.

China is still a communist country (which the United States once saw as a threat) and has repeatedly stated its objective of destroying the United States. Why are we paying for our own destruction? Some will say China is an enemy only if we force them to be an enemy. They say Free Trade with China will end communism in China the way the arms race forced bankruptcy and ended communism in the Soviet Union. That may be true, but why risk the stability of the United States on it?

Once we accept the reality that the United States government believes Free Trade with China is Good for the USA, and that we the people cannot easily change that, we must review the possible outcomes of that policy. If we continue to import billions of dollars in goods every year from China, the Chinese people will certainly benefit. Incomes will rise and their standard of living will improve. They will be exposed to the freedoms that we in America take for granted.

Today, millions of Chinese citizens are employed by foreign companies in partnership with Chinese companies and the communist government. Many companies are already seeing a shortage of qualified workers. This has caused an average annual rise in salaries of approximately ten percent. Of course, the average salary of a semi-skilled laborer is still only a few hundred dollars per month. It will take a very long time to catch up to middle-class wages in the United States. The short-term result of the labor shortage is a huge investment in education to ensure that the next generation of Chinese citizens will be qualified to take advantage of the jobs available.

Over time, the people will demand more freedom from their government, and the government will be forced to respond. In fact, some rural areas are already holding rudimentary elections, with candidates from parties other than the communist party. The national communist party is allowing these elections to take place. As they spread, the government can be expected to limit election freedoms or risk losing control of the people and eventually causing the communist party to dissolve. The theory of "Buy Chinese" claims the communist government will fall, and democracy will take route in China, making the world a safer place.

Before this optimistic scenario can occur, China must form a viable economy of its own.

China will need much more investment from the capitalist world. That's where we come in. Buy Chinese goods and help end communism in China. It won't take billions of dollars. It will take trillions of dollars. Trillions of dollars pulled from our domestic economy and shipped off to China in exchange for chairs and desks and lamps and hundreds of other depreciating products.

Perhaps, this shipping of U.S. dollars to China really will eventually end communism. It appears to be filled with danger and risk, but maybe it's better than a Soviet-style arms race. Most Americans old enough to remember the Cuban Missile Crisis and the decades of peril that followed probably weren't fully convinced that the policy of mutually assured destruction was the right way for our government to defeat Soviet Communism.

So, for the purpose of this book, let's assume the United States government does expect to end Communism in China by flooding that country with capitalism. Why not do the same thing in Cuba and North Korea? Have the high thinkers in our government thought through the varied possible outcomes of their plan?

We'll probably never know the answers to those questions, but we can look at what's happening in China today and theorize what it could mean to our future. As expected, China does not play by

American business rules. Yes, they have joined several global organizations and promised to reform past problems; however, Chinese promises are not always trustworthy.

Copyright and trademark infringement are popular activities in China. The government says they are cracking down on the people responsible for the problem, but year after year, things seem to stay the same. If you want the latest movie on DVD, you can often buy it for less than a dollar on Chinese street corners a few days after the United States launch. Countless American businesses have complained about government sanctioned (or at least government ignored) copyright infringement. They are told China will reform and in time, copyrights will have the protection that members of the WTO have promised.

China's predatory business practices go beyond copyright issues. In 2004, General Motors filed a complaint with the Chinese authorities regarding technology theft in a Chinese produced car. GM claimed the Chery QQ model was an illegal copy of the Chevrolet Spark. According to a General Motors spokesperson, "It's such a knockoff that you can pull a door off of the Chevy *Spark* and it fits on the QQ - and it fits so well that the seals on the door hold." Chinese Deputy Commerce Minister Zhang Zhigang determined that GM did not prove its case against Chery and the Chery QQ has since won market share in China by outselling the Chevy Spark.

Chery is a government owned car manufacturer in China. Chevrolet designed the Spark exclusively for the Chinese market and manufactured it in China with Chinese business partners and Chinese workers. Less than a year after it was introduced, Chery (not Chevy . . . Chery) offered the QQ for $3,500, a full $1,000 cheaper than the Spark. That's right, China has the Chery—that looks exactly like the Chevy—for only $3,500. Of course, Chery isn't planning to offer $3,500 cars in the United States. They have announced that they will price their cars in the $19,000 range. These $19,000 cars won't compete with existing low cost cars. They will target customers of $30,000 cars. They will enjoy higher profits on $19,000 cars than domestic and global car companies earn on $30,000 cars. All because of a huge savings in labor and benefit costs. How this new competition will affect U.S. auto workers will depend on the response of American buyers. In 2017, Chery sells the QQ3, QQ6 and QQev in China, Iran, Malaysia and other countries that don't have strict safety requirements.

General Motors has invested huge sums of money in China with hopes of benefiting from the gigantic future consumer market. The key word is "future." Hundreds of American companies have—and are—investing in China in an effort to earn future profits from that promised consumer market. So far, the Chery QQ and similarly produced products are winning.

It's not only General Motors that has met Chinese business practices head on. Knockoffs have been found for many other cars. China has the Chery car company to copy America's Chevy, and China's Hongda car company has copied Honda cars. Chrysler has also had experience with Chinese car companies.

In 1995, Chrysler was building 4-wheel drive Jeep Cherokees at a Chinese Army auto manufacturing plant. Yes, the Chinese army. Why an American company would build vehicles with help from the Chinese army is a topic for another book that might be entitled, "Are We Stupid, or What?" But here, we just want to look at the cost to American jobs.

Chrysler was building these Jeeps for the Chinese army and Chinese consumers at an army-owned manufacturing plant. It didn't take long before Chrysler saw knockoffs of the Jeep on Chinese roads. The Chinese government accepted Chrysler's complaints and did nothing to stop the obvious theft. Chrysler soon decided not to go forward with a planned auto manufacturing plant in Shanghai.

Fast forward to 2017, and Fiat Chrysler has plans to manufacture the Jeep, and other cars, in China for the Chinese market. In April, 2016, Fiat Chrysler proudly announced its plans to increase investment with Chinese auto partners. In the United States, Fiat Chrysler and all other companies don't need partners. In China, it's mandatory. The partner is often the Chinese government.

In the United States, companies make deals with other companies. The government does not own a piece of the deal. In China, foreign companies must negotiate directly or indirectly with the government or its representatives. When General Motors wanted to build a manufacturing plant in China to build cars for the Chinese market, they had to get government approval. To get that approval, they were told to quickly increase sourcing of car components from Chinese companies for American-made cars and to help China become a technological leader in car manufacturing. General Motors agreed, and China is rapidly gaining the expertise to build world-class automobiles.

It is important to mention that most other car manufacturers and car part manufacturers have made similar deals with China's communist government. China's well-planned economic strategy is not focused on its domestic market. It is focused on the export market. Companies that want access to China's domestic market must put their international future at risk by helping China to become a global leader.

A sobering example is China's deal with Boeing. Boeing, based in Seattle, Washington, is one of the two global leaders in commercial aircraft production. China has systematically played Boeing and Airbus (its European competitor) against each other in an effort to extract technological know-how. Chinese airlines have ordered dozens of Boeing's aircraft worth billions of dollars. In exchange for the business, Boeing has agreed to source an ever-increasing number of components from Chinese firms. In 2015, Boeing announced it will build its first overseas aircraft manufacturing facility in China. The deal with Chinese state-owned companies gives Boeing greater access to the Chinese market for commuter aircraft.

These types of deals are called "offsets." Offsets are a way for a government to pressure companies to shift manufacturing to the country in exchange for access to the country's market. Offsets are expressly forbidden by China's WTO agreement. China negotiates offsets in virtually every industry. With the Boeing deals, China gains access to important aircraft manufacturing technologies, Boeing gains access to the Chinese market and the United States loses high paying aircraft manufacturing jobs.

Boeing may not end up the winner in this deal, after all. China Aviation Industry Corporation has a commuter jet called the ARJ21. Various American companies are working with the Chinese company by supplying engines and other high-tech components for the ARJ21. This jet is expected to capture a meaningful share of the Chinese commuter jet market and eventually compete with Boeing and others in the global market. It received approval from the Chinese government to sell in the Chinese market in 2016. It's application for approval with the U.S. FAA is currently under review.

Instead of investing page after page in examples of China's poor business ethics, it might be wiser to turn to U.S. government reports:

> In line with China's industrial policies, foreign investment into some sectors has shifted from encouraged to restricted or even prohibited.

> These fluctuations in China's foreign investment restrictions reflect a pattern whereby the government welcomes FDI into sectors designated as strategic for China's national economic development in order to extract technology and other advantages from foreign firms. However, after domestic industry is deemed sufficiently developed, policies welcoming investment are gradually withdrawn and new policies restricting investment are put in place to free up market space for domestic firms and push out foreign firms.

The previous quote was taken directly from the 2015 "**REPORT TO CONGRESS** *of the* U.S.-CHINA ECONOMIC AND SECURITY REVIEW COMMISSION" released in November 2015. Each year, the commission researches and reports on the relationship between the United States and China. After reading the nearly six-hundred-page report, it becomes clear that the United States government is not doing enough to protect our nation's economic future from unfair Chinese business practices. It also states:

> China causes increasing harm to the U.S. economy and

security through two deliberate policies targeting the United States: coordinated, government-backed theft of information from a wide variety of U.S.-based commercial enterprises and widespread restrictions on content, standards, and commercial opportunities for U.S. businesses. Hackers working for the Chinese government—or with the government's support and encouragement—have infiltrated the computer networks of U.S. government agencies, contractors, and private companies, and stolen personal information and trade secrets.

The report declares that China has a well-thought-out plan for dealing with the United States. It also points out that the United States does not have a plan for dealing with China. The words on most pages almost beg the government to do something . . . anything.

The report has been submitted to Congress each year since 2003. Surprisingly, the conclusions are quite similar each year, with stern warnings to Congress about China's business and global activities. The biggest change in the report is that it was three hundred pages long in 2005 and, ten years later in 2015, it was six hundred pages long.

China undervalues its currency. This helps keep the cost of Chinese goods low and also acts to bar U.S. exports to China. The end result is that China's purposefully undervalued currency influences U.S. companies to close their facilities in the United States and move production to China.

In 2002, China was given conditional membership in the World Trade Organization (WTO). The WTO is a global organization, supported by member nations. It acts as the guardian and arbitrator of acceptable global business practices. When China joined the WTO, it agreed to make many changes in its business methods. Today, China has failed to make many of the most important changes. The areas that China has not reformed, include its practice of extensive subsidies for state-owned companies, its weak intellectual property rights and its labor practices. The WTO clearly declared that China must change if it wants to be an accepted part of the global economy.

So far, the WTO has proven to be mostly talk with very little action. China continues to enjoy a strong advantage versus the industrialized nations of the world. It has been served with antidumping duties on several occasions; however, those duties remain mostly uncollected. Every year that goes by without a plan to genuinely deal with China, means more jobs lost and more American industries harmed.

China has used its advantage to great benefit. The United States Department of Defense (DoD) will face increasingly difficult procurement problems in the near future. Military component suppliers are moving much of their production out of the United States. Since the U.S. military does not own any manufacturers (as the Chinese military does), the DoD must purchase microchips and virtually all other supplies and equipment from independent companies. When these companies source their products from China, it adds a new level of risk to military procurements.

In the area of energy, China is spreading the money it earns from American consumers all over the world. It is buying energy at the wellhead, instead of on the open market like most of the world's nations. The 2015 report also sates:

President Xi came to the United States in September (2015) on a state visit and although Presidents Obama and Xi discussed several issues of concern, including commercial cyber espionage by Chinese actors, there were few significant breakthroughs. Among outcomes were the statements by the two presidents that neither country will engage in cyber espionage (though China continued to deny any involvement in commercial cyber theft) and commitments to enhance cooperation on combatting climate change.

Read the above quote again. As high-paying jobs disappear and we lose our manufacturing base, American workers will have to accept lower-paying jobs. Less money means fewer purchases and, eventually, a lower standard of living. While this happens, our leaders discuss increased cooperation on climate change.

Henry Ford believed his workers should be able to afford the car that they built. In the early 1900s, Henry Ford paid his workers the unheard of salary of $5 per day. This gave them the ability to buy the Model T cars they were building. The Chinese government doesn't believe its employees should be able to afford the products they build, but it does agree with Henry Ford in one way . . . many Chinese workers earn just $5 per day.

So it appears China is about one hundred years behind the salary curve, but right up to date in technological ability. The Commission's report points out that the movement of manufacturing jobs to China is paralleled by transfers of technology. Many research centers are being opened in China every year. The potential and probable impact on our future competitive ability is enormous. The time to act is now, because as the United States economy becomes more dependent on Chinese capital and Chinese products, the ability to effectively act diminishes. Nobody knows if we have already reached the, "It's now or never" stage of the U.S.-China relationship, but it's clear to many that the time is near.

In the 2015 "**REPORT TO CONGRESS** *of the* U.S.-CHINA ECONOMIC AND SECURITY REVIEW COMMISSION", the commissioners seem to be begging the United States government to do something about China. They want a strategic plan for dealing with China that takes into account the grave threat to the U.S. standard of living that China presents. Occasionally, we read in the newspapers about how the government is getting tough with China, but there's still no stated strategy. It seems the "Buy Chinese" theory rules the day.

In the final chapters of the report, the commissioners added personal comments. Some of those comments follow:

"We must stop simply hoping for the best or China's reformation to Western ideals. Rather, we must deal with the hard reality of the unique characteristics of state-led capitalism."

"The critical juncture we face is whether a more realistic, pragmatic, self-interested and self-assured policy will be advanced by U.S. government officials or whether they will continue to engage in endless dialogue while U.S. economic and security interests continue to be undermined."

"Nothing about China is certain, but it clearly is time to stop giving China's leaders the benefit of the doubt. Their actions to this point don't justify it, and worse days may well be coming."

If trading with China eventually ends communism in China, what will it mean to the United States? It is possible that China's economy will become self-sufficient and prosperity in China will spread throughout the country. With 1.3 billion citizens, China is four times the size of the United States; therefore, their economy will have to grow to four times that of the United States to equal our prosperity and standard of living.

An economy of that size will demand huge amounts of energy and raw materials. The Chinese reaction to an incredibly successful, self-sufficient domestic economy could cause them to reduce exports so they can satisfy demand in their own country. If the United States has reduced its manufacturing base to a critical level, prices for all types of goods will skyrocket and inflation will surge. This would not be good for the average American.

Now, if China reaches this level of success before the communist party loses power, the result could be even worse. China could simply cut off the United States and refuse to supply us with the items we desperately need. This would be devastating to the U.S. economy.

Many politicians say there's no need to worry about either of these scenarios yet. They believe China relies on the United States just as much as we rely on them. Without easy access to the U.S. market, China could not maintain its strong growth.

> . . . China's dependence on the American marketplace for the sale of its products and as a source of investment and technology is so large as to make China's economic growth to a substantial extent dependent on the American economy. This provides the United States with enormous leverage to demand that China adopt greater reforms and

abandon its mercantilist practices.

This statement was on page 22 of the Commission's nearly 300-page report from 2005. The 2015 report does not mention ". . . China's dependence on the American marketplace . . . " It does, however, mention, " . . . the dependence of the national security industrial base of the United States on imports from China . . . "

CHAPTER SIX

GLOBAL BRAND RATINGS

The following pages are supplied as a guide to help American consumers select the products that best help American workers. The ratings are presented for more than 300 global brands in the following categories. Each category lists the complete brand ratings from high to low and in alphabetical order. Between the high to low and alphabetical ratings, you'll find profiles of two companies.

Audio & Video Products

The Audio and Video category includes global brands that offer everything from televisions and radios to headsets and game consoles.

The highest-rated brand earns 161 *Good for the USA* points. The lowest comes in at -20 and happens to be a U.S. based company that imports all of its products. The highest-rated foreign brand is Clarion at 56 points.

Well-known brands rated above 50 points include Bose, Clarion, GoPro, JBL and Magnavox. Famous brands rated below zero points include Cambridge, JVC, Kenwood, Philips and RCA.

Following are the complete brand ratings from high to low and in alphabetical order. Between the high to low and alphabetical ratings, you'll find profiles of two companies.

Audio & Video Products
(Highest to Lowest Rating)

Brand	Rating	Notes
Amazon	161	
Insignia	161	
Microsoft	125	
Apple	118	
Beats by Dre	118	

Brand	Rating	Notes
Google	100	
Bose	70	
AKG	67	
Harman Kardon	67	
JBL	67	
Kodak	64	
Nvidia	61	
Clarion	56	
Hitachi	56	
Magnavox	54	
GoPro	52	
Koss	50	
Sony	44	
Samsung	37	
Panasonic	34	
A-Audio	30	

Brand	Rating	Notes
Definitive Technology	30	
Polk Audio	30	
Tivoli Audio	30	
ZVOX	30	
Garmin	26	
Sennheiser	25	
Sceptre	20	
Yamaha	15	
Nintendo	13	
Sharp	13	
Canon	6	
Haier	5	
Bang & Olufsen	2	
Vizio	2	
OPPO	0	
PSB	0	

Brand	Rating	Notes
Audio-Technica	-10	
ION Audio	-10	
Parrot	-11	
Philips	-11	
TCL	-11	
Cambridge Audio	-15	
LG	-15	
JVC	-19	
Kenwood	-19	
Phiaton	-19	
Audiovox	-20	
Kitvision	-20	
Klipsch	-20	
RCA	-20	

Eastman Kodak Company

The Eastman Kodak Company occupied a leading position in imaging technology for more than a century since its founding by George Eastman and Henry A. Strong in 1888. In the 1980s, the company employed more than 145,000 people worldwide, with more than 60,000 in the United States. Since then, rapidly changing technology and increasing competition had forced Eastman Kodak into bankruptcy in 2012 and to just 2,800 U.S. employees in 2016.

This is not a story of offshoring of jobs. Eastman Kodak has been struggling to survive in a changing world. The company licensed or sold many of its patents to others and has revised its product offerings several times. You will see the Kodak name on products from several unaffiliated companies, but Eastman Kodak emerged from bankruptcy in 2013 and is working to build a new future for the iconic American brand.

Year Founded:	1888
Country:	United States
Global Employees:	6,400
U.S. Employees:	2,800 (44%)
Global Sales:	$1.8 billion
U.S. Sales:	$622 million (35%)

Good for the USA Rating:

1) Headquarters:	USA	20 pts.
2) % U.S. employees (44) minus % U.S. sales (35) plus 50		59 pts.
3) 2,800 U.S. employees		-15 pts.
4) U.S. Manufacturing:	YES	0 pts.
5) Foreign Manufacturing:	YES	0 pts.
Total Points		64 Points

Garmin Ltd

Garmin was founded in the United States in Lenexa, Kansas in 1989 by Gary Burrell and Min H. Kao. The company name was derived from the first three letters of the founders' first names; GAR from Gary Burrell and Min from Min H. Kao. They incorporated their company in Taiwan, and their first major customer was the United States Army.

In 2000, they moved the recorded headquarters to the Cayman Islands because Taiwan incorporation didn't benefit a planned stock offering in the United States. In 2010, they transferred incorporation to Switzerland to offer more opportunities for expansion in Europe.

Executive offices are still located in Olathe, Kansas. Today, the United Sates remains Garmin's biggest market, but they are, due to place of incorporation, a foreign company.

Year Founded:	1989
Country:	Switzerland
Global Employees:	11,651
U.S. Employees:	4,333 (37%)
Global Sales:	$2.8 billion
U.S. Sales:	$1.3 billion (46%)

Good for the USA Rating:

1) Headquarters:	Switzerland	0 pts.
2) % U.S. employees (37) minus % U.S. sales (46) plus 50		41 pts.
3) 4,333 U.S. employees		-15 pts.
4) U.S. Manufacturing:	YES	0 pts.
5) Foreign Manufacturing:	YES	0 pts.
Total Points		26 Points

Audio & Video Products
(Alphabetical Order)

Brand	Rating	Notes
A-Audio	30	
AKG	67	
Amazon	161	
Apple	118	
Audio-Technica	-10	
Audiovox	-20	
Bang & Olufsen	2	
Beats by Dre	118	
Bose	70	
Cambridge Audio	-15	
Canon	6	
Clarion	56	
Definitive Technology	30	
Garmin	26	
Google	100	

Brand	Rating	Notes
GoPro	52	
Haier	5	
Harman Kardon	67	
Hitachi	56	
Insignia	161	
ION	-10	
JBL	67	
JVC	-19	
Kenwood	-19	
Kitvision	-20	
Klipsch	-20	
Kodak	64	
Koss	50	
LG	-15	
Magnavox	54	
Microsoft	125	

Brand	Rating	Notes
Nintendo	13	
Nvidia	61	
OPPO	0	
Panasonic	34	
Parrot	-11	
Phiaton	-19	
Philips	-11	
Polk Audio	30	
PSB	0	
RCA	-20	
Samsung	37	
Sceptre	20	
Sennheiser	25	
Sharp	13	
Sony	44	
TCL	-11	

Brand	Rating	Notes
Tivoli Audio	30	
Vizio	2	
Yamaha	15	
ZVOX	30	

Baby Products

The Baby Products category includes brands that offer products for babies and young children. The brands listed include very large brands such as Disney and relatively small, privately-owned brands. During our research, we found some brands that went out of business and then came back under the same ownership as a new brand.

Most companies own multiple brands. Disney owns Disney, InStep and Coco. U.S.-based Carter's, Inc. owns Carter's, OshKosh B'Gosh, Precious First, Child of Mine, Just One You and Genuine Kids. And China-based Goodbaby International Holdings, Lmt. owns ExcerSaucer, Evenflo, Rollplay, CYBEX and Urbini.

As with all brands rated in *Good for the USA*, you should do your research, select two or three brands you would like to consider, and then see which brand gets the best rating. Then share your purchase on social media and tell the world that *Good for the USA* tipped the choice to the brand you bought and away from your runners-up.

Following are the complete brand ratings from high to low and in alphabetical order. Between the high to low and alphabetical ratings, you'll find profiles of two companies.

Baby Products
(Highest to Lowest Rating)

Brand	Rating	Notes
Coco	195	
Disney	195	

Brand	Rating	Notes
InStep	195	
Pottery Barn Kids	84	
Carter's	54	
Child of Mine	54	
Genuine Kids	54	
Just One You	54	
OshKosh B'gosh	54	
Precious Firsts	54	
Maxi-Cosi	46	
Quinny	46	
Safety 1st	46	
4moms	40	
Baby Einstein	38	
Bright Starts	38	
Anka	30	
Aprica	30	

Brand	Rating	Notes
Baby Caché	30	
Baby Mod	30	
Babyletto	30	
Baby's Dream	30	
BÉABA	30	
Bloom	30	
Cariboo	30	
DaVinci	30	
Graco	30	
Kolcraft	30	
LÍLLÉbaby	30	
Micralite	30	
Nursery Works	30	
SVAN	30	
American Girl	2	
Fishher-Price	2	

Brand	Rating	Notes
AP Industries	0	
CYBEX	-7	
Evenflo	-7	
ExcerSaucer	-7	
Goodbaby	-7	
Rollplay	-7	
Urbini	-7	
BabyBjörn	-25	

Dorel Industries

Dorel Industries is a Canada-based company that owns many baby product brands including Safety 1st, Quinny, Maxi-Cosi and Tiny Love. They also own Dorel Sports brands including Cannondale, Schwinn, GT, Mongoose, Caloi, IronHorse and SUGOI.

Dorel Industries has maintained many jobs in the United States, but they have also shifted many jobs in bicycle manufacturing to China and other countries in recent years. If this continues, their strong *Good for the USA* rating will begin to drop. With fifty-four percent of their sales coming from buyers in the United States, Dorel Industries should be motivated to keep as many jobs in the United States as possible.

Year Founded:	1962
Country:	Canada
Global Employees:	10,450
U.S. Employees:	5,200 (50%)
Global Sales:	$2.7 billion
U.S. Sales:	$1.46 billion (54%)

Good for the USA Rating:

1) Headquarters:	Canada	0 pts.
2) % U.S. employees (50) minus % U.S. sales (54) plus 50		46 pts.
3) 5,200 U.S. employees		0 pts.
4) U.S. Manufacturing:	YES	0 pts.
5) Foreign Manufacturing:	YES	0 pts.
Total Points		46 Points

Goodbaby International Holdings, Ltd.

Goodbaby International Holdings, Ltd. owns several baby and juvenile brands including Goodbaby, GB, CYBEX, Evenflo, CBX, Rollplay, Happy Dino and Urbini. The company was founded in 1989 by Zhenghuan Song when he designed a children's rocking chair. In 2014, Goodbaby purchased the CYBEX and Evenflo (ExerSaucer) brands to expand its image in the United States and Europe. Fully, forty percent of Goodbaby's sales come from the United States.

While the company does claim some U.S. manufacturing, the great majority of its products are imported into the United States. Most of its manufacturing facilities are based in China.

Year Founded:	1989
Country:	China
Global Employees:	12,318
U.S. Employees:	400 (3%)
Global Sales:	$903.6 million
U.S. Sales:	$364.6 million (40%)

Good for the USA Rating:

1) Headquarters:	China	0 pts.
2) % U.S. employees (3) minus % U.S. sales (40) plus 50		13 pts.
3) 400 U.S. employees:		-20 pts.
4) U.S. Manufacturing:	YES	0 pts.
5) Foreign Manufacturing	YES	0 pts.
Total Points		-7 Points

Baby Products
(Alphabetical Order)

Brand	Rating	Notes
4moms	40	
American Girl	2	
Anka	30	
AP Industries	0	
Aprica	30	
BabyBjörn	-25	
Baby Caché	30	
Baby Einstein	38	
Babyletto	30	
Baby Mod	30	
Baby's Dream	30	
BÉABA	30	
Bloom	30	
Bright Starts	38	
Cariboo	30	

Brand	Rating	Notes
Carter's	54	
Child of Mine	54	
Coco	195	
CYBEX	-7	
DaVinci	30	
Disney	195	
Evenflo	-7	
ExcerSaucer	-7	
Fisher-Price	2	
Genuine Kids	54	
Goodbaby	-7	
Graco	30	
InStep	195	
Just One You	54	
Kolcraft	30	
LÍLLÉbaby	30	

Brand	Rating	Notes
Maxi-Cosi	46	
Micralite	30	
Nurseryworks	30	
OshKosh B'gosh	54	
Pottery Barn Kids	84	
Precious Firsts	54	
Quinny	46	
Rollplay	-7	
Safety 1st	46	
SVAN	30	
Urbini	-7	

Bicycles/Exercise Equipment

The Bicycle and Exercise Equipment section shows ratings from a high of 85 *Good for the USA* points to a low of -20. The bicycle brands are interesting because many of the well-known brands are owned by foreign-based companies with strong ratings. For instance, Cannondale, Mongoose and Schwinn bicycles are all owned by a Canadian company that has fifty percent of their employees in the USA.

Often, when we see foreign companies with a high percentage of their employees in the U.S., it's because they purchased American companies and decided to keep the factories open. This makes it important to tell these companies that you bought their brand because they support American workers.

The exercise-related products range from highly-rated American brands including NordicTrack, Cybex and Fitbit to low-rated foreign brands such as Horizon Fitness and LiveStrong.

As with all brands rated in *Good for the USA*, you should do your research, select two or three brands you would like to consider, and then see which brand gets the best rating. Then, share your purchase on social media and tell the world that *Good for the USA* tipped the choice to the brand you bought and away from your runners-up.

Following are the complete brand ratings from high to low and in alphabetical order. Between the high to low and alphabetical ratings, you'll find profiles of two companies.

Bicycles & Exercise Equipment
(Highest to Lowest Rating)

Brand	Rating	Notes
NordicTrack	85	
ProForm	85	
Cybex	70	
Hammer Strength	70	
InMovement	70	
Life Fitness	70	
Fitbit	48	
Cannondale	46	
Mongoose	46	
Schwinn	46	
Withings	31	
Diamondback	25	
Raleigh	25	
BH	-10	

Brand	Rating	Notes
Advanced Fitness Group	-15	
Horizon Fitness	-15	
LiveStrong	-15	
Vision	-15	
Kettler	-20	

Nokia Corporation

Nokia Corporation was once among the largest mobile phone manufacturers in the world. The company lost its leadership role and found itself nearing bankruptcy. It sold the Nokia brand name for mobile phones to Microsoft in 2014. In May, 2016, Microsoft sold the name to HMD Global, a newly-formed company with ties to Foxconn, a Chinese manufacturer.

Nokia Corporation purchased Withings, a French consumer electronics company in April, 2016 and merged the connected health devices into its new Digital Health division. So if you see a product branded Withings, it is actually from Nokia, but if you see a mobile phone branded Nokia, it's probably from a Chinese company.

Year Founded:	1865
Country:	Finland
Global Employees:	56,690
U.S. Employees:	3,813 (7%)
Global Sales:	$14.1 billion
U.S. Sales:	$1.6 billion (11%)

Good for the USA Rating:

1) Headquarters:	Finland	0 pts.
2) % U.S. employees (7) minus % U.S. sales (11) plus 50		46 pts.
3) 3,813 U.S. employees		-15 pts.
4) U.S. Manufacturing:	YES	0 pts.
5) Foreign Manufacturing:	YES	0 pts.
Total Points		31 Points

Johnson Health Tech Co., Ltd.

Johnson Health Tech Co., Ltd. sounds like an American name, but it's not. JHT was founded in 1975 in Taiwan by Peter Lo. He started his company by writing letters to 1,000 American companies asking them if his company could help them with manufacturing. Only three responded, but that was enough to get his company started in the exercise equipment market.

After focusing only on the U.S. market, JHT has expanded to twenty-six worldwide subsidiaries.

The company's brands include Advanced Fitness Group, Horizon Fitness, LiveStrong and Vision.

Year Founded: 1975
Country: Taiwan
Global Employees: 10,000
U.S. Employees: 280 (3%)
Global Sales: $500 million
U.S. Sales: $139 million (28%)

Good for the USA Rating:

1) Headquarters:	Taiwan	0 pts.
2) % U.S. employees (3) minus % U.S. sales (28) plus 50		25 pts.
3) 280 U.S. employees		-20 pts.
4) U.S. Manufacturing:	NO	-20 pts.
5) Foreign Manufacturing:	YES	0 pts.
Total Points		-15 Points

Bicycles & Exercise Equipment
(Alphabetical Order)

Brand	Rating	Notes
Advanced Fitness Group	-15	
BH	-10	
Cannondale	46	
Cybex	70	
Diamondback	25	
Fitbit	48	
Hammer Strength	70	
Horizon Fitness	-15	
InMovement	70	
Kettler	-20	
Life Fitness	70	
LiveStrong	-15	
Mongoose	46	
NordicTrack	85	

Brand	Rating	Notes
ProForm	85	
Raleigh	25	
Schwinn	46	
Vision	-15	
Withings	31	

Boats & Water Products

Most of the brands in the Boats and Water Products section are owned by U.S. companies. Only one brand in this category earned a negative rating. The rest rated higher with Brunswick Corporation owning more than half the major brands.

There are several relatively small boat manufacturers that have made their boats in the USA with American workers for decades.

As with all brands rated in *Good for the USA*, you should do your research, select two or three brands you would like to consider, and then see which brand gets the best rating. Then, share your purchase on social media and tell the world that *Good for the USA* tipped the choice to the brand you bought and away from your runners-up.

Following are the complete brand ratings from high to low and in alphabetical order. Between the high to low and alphabetical ratings, you'll find profiles of two companies.

Boats & Water Products
(Highest to Lowest Rating)

Brand	Rating	Notes
Regal	90	
Chaparral	81	
Robalo	81	
MasterCraft	80	

Brand	Rating	Notes
Attwood	70	
Bayliner	70	
Bell Industries RPG	70	
Boston Whaler	70	
Crestliner	70	
Cypress Cay	70	
Diversified Marine	70	
Grady-White	70	
Harris	70	
Kellogg Marine	70	
Land 'N' Sea	70	
Lowe Boats	70	
Lund	70	
Mariner	70	
Mercury	70	
Meridian Yachts	70	

Brand	Rating	Notes
MotorGuide	70	
Princecraft	70	
Quicksilver	70	
Sea Ray	70	
SmartCraft	70	
Swivl-Eze	70	
Thunder Jet	70	
Whale	70	
Black & Decker	48	
Malibu Boats	47	
Bosch	14	
Bertram	9	
Four Winns	7	
Wellcraft	7	
Yamaha Boats	-8	

Malibu Boats

Malibu Boats was founded in 1982 by a group of friends. Today, the company is based in Loudon, Tennessee. Most of its employees (87%) and sales (90%) are in the United States.

They have consistently been respected as one of the leading boat makers in the United States.

They have a small operation in Australia.

Malibu Boats is one of several U.S.-based boat manufacturers that have maintained manufacturing in the United States for many decades.

Year Founded:	1982
Country:	United States
Global Employees:	509
U.S. Employees:	445 (87%)
Global Sales:	$228.6 million
U.S. Sales:	$205.7 million (90%)

Good for the USA Rating:

1) Headquarters:	USA	20 pts.
2) % U.S. employees (87) minus % U.S. sales (90) plus 50		47 pts.
3) 445 U.S. employees		-20 pts.
4) U.S. Manufacturing:	YES	0 pts.
5) Foreign Manufacturing:	YES	0 pts.
Total Points		47 Points

Marine Products Corporation

Marine Products Corporation manufactures Chaparral Boats and Robalo Boats. The company is based in Atlanta, Georgia. It traces its origin back to 1965 when Chaparral Boats were first made. In 2001, they purchased the assets of Robalo Boats, which was ceasing production after more than thirty years. Next, Chaparral and Robalo Boats were united under the Marine Products Corporation name.

MPC sells their boats throughout the world, but one hundred percent of their employees are based in Georgia.

Year Founded:	1965
Country:	United States
Global Employees:	767
U.S. Employees:	767 (100%)
Global Sales:	$207 million
U.S. Sales:	$184.8 million (89%)

Good for the USA Rating:

1) Headquarters:	USA	20 pts.
2) % U.S. employees (47) minus % U.S. sales (55) plus 50		61 pts.
3) 767 U.S. employees		-20 pts.
4) U.S. Manufacturing:	YES	0 pts.
5) Foreign Manufacturing:	NO	20 pts.
Total Points		81 Points

Boats & Water Products
(Alphabetical Order)

Brand	Rating	Notes
Attwood	70	
Bayliner	70	
Bell Industries RPG	70	
Bertram	9	
Black & Decker	48	
Bosch	14	
Boston Whaler	70	
Chaparral	81	
Crestliner	70	
Cypress Cay	70	
Diversified Marine	70	
Four Winns	7	
Grady-White	70	
Harris	70	
Kellogg Marine	70	

Brand	Rating	Notes
Land 'N' Sea	70	
Lowe Boats	70	
Lund	70	
Malibu Boats	47	
Mariner	70	
MasterCraft	80	
Mercury	70	
Meridian Yachts	70	
MotorGuide	70	
Princecraft	70	
Quicksilver	70	
Regal	90	
Robalo	81	
Sea Ray	70	
SmartCraft	70	
Swivl-Eze	70	

Brand	Rating	Notes
Thunder Jet	70	
Wellcraft	7	
Whale	70	
Yamaha Boats	-8	

Cameras

The Camera category includes many well-known brands. It does not include the mobile phone brands that all have very capable cameras. Sony, Pentax and Ricoh are the highest-rated foreign brands. On quality lists, Nikon will rate at or near the top, but on the *Good for the USA* list they rank at the bottom.

As with all brands rated in *Good for the USA*, you should do your research, select two or three brands you would like to consider, and then see which brand gets the best rating. Then, share your purchase on social media and tell the world that *Good for the USA* tipped the choice to the brand you bought and away from your runners-up.

Following are the complete brand ratings from high to low and in alphabetical order. Between the high to low and alphabetical ratings, you'll find profiles of two companies.

Cameras
(Highest to Lowest Rating)

Brand	Rating	Notes
Microsoft	125	
Google	100	
GoPro	52	
Sony	44	
Pentax	41	

Brand	Rating	Notes
Ricoh	41	
Panasonic	34	
Olympus	16	
Canon	6	
Asus	-6	
Nikon	-15	

Ricoh Company, Ltd.

Ricoh Company, Ltd. was founded in Japan in 1936 as Riken Sensitized Paper. Today, the company's brands include Ricoh, Pentax, Lanier, Gestetner and Savin.

Ricoh currently has about 40,000 of its 109,400 employees in Japan. The rest are positioned in 180 countries around the world. Locations for employees are in part determined by the growth potential in each country. This has resulted in about 15,000 American jobs, or fourteen percent of the Ricoh workforce. Since they earn twenty-eight percent of their sales from the United States, there may be room for jobs growth.

Year Founded:	1936
Country:	Japan
Global Employees:	109,400
U.S. Employees:	15,000 (14%)
Global Sales:	2.2 billion Yen
U.S. Sales:	625 million Yen (28%)

Good for the USA Rating:

1) Headquarters:	Japan	0 pts.
2) % U.S. employees (14) minus % U.S. sales (28) plus 50		36 pts.
3) 15,000 U.S. employees		5 pts.
4) U.S. Manufacturing:	YES	0 pts.
5) Foreign Manufacturing:	YES	0 pts.
Total Points		41 Points

Sony Corporation

Sony was founded in 1946 as an electronics shop in a Tokyo department store building. It was originally called Tokyo Tsushin Kogyo. The name was changed to Sony in 1958 in an effort to make the name more memorable for American consumers. Sony was selected as a combination of "sonus", the Latin root for sound and "sonny", a 1950s American slang term for calling a boy.

Sony has frequently reset its corporate structure and re-positioned its workforce to align with global corporate strategies. This has led to loss of jobs and gains of jobs over recent years.

Year Founded: 1946
Country: Japan
Global Employees: 125,300
U.S. Employees: 13,783 (11%)
Global Sales: $71.7 billion
U.S. Sales: $15.3 billion (21%)

Good for the USA Rating:

1) Headquarters:	Japan	0 pts.
2) % U.S. employees (11) minus % U.S. sales (21) plus 50		40 pts.
3) 13,783 U.S. employees		4 pts.
4) U.S. Manufacturing:	YES	0 pts.
5) Foreign Manufacturing:	YES	0 pts.
Total Points		44 Points

Cameras
(Alphabetical Order)

Brand	Rating	Notes
Asus	-6	
Canon	6	
Google	100	
GoPro	52	
Microsoft	125	
Nikon	-15	
Olympus	16	
Panasonic	34	
Pentax	41	
Ricoh	41	
Sony	44	

Cars

The car category is unique in that most major global manufacturers have a manufacturing facility in the United States. Honda has twelve manufacturing facilities in the U.S. They claim they have manufactured 22.4 million cars in the U.S. since 1982 and have exported 1.1 million cars from the U.S. since 1987; however, they also make cars in Mexico for export into the U.S. When a car company chooses a location for a new plant, many factors go into the decision.

Their choice can be influenced by the U.S. President and by U.S. consumers.

As with all brands rated in *Good for the USA*, you should do your research, select two or three brands you would like to consider, and then see which brand gets the best rating. Then, share your purchase on social media and tell the world that *Good for the USA* tipped the choice to the brand you bought and away from your runners-up.

Following are the complete brand ratings from high to low and in alphabetical order. Between the high to low and alphabetical ratings, you'll find profiles of two companies.

Cars
(Highest to Lowest Rating)

Brand	Rating	Notes
Buick	140	
Cadillac	140	

Brand	Rating	Notes
Chevrolet	140	
GMC	140	
Tesla	122	
Ford	88	
Lincoln	88	
Alfa Romeo	64	
Chrysler	64	
Dodge	64	
Fiat	64	
Jeep	64	
Maserati	64	
Ram	64	
Genesis	45	
Hyundai	45	
MINI	39	
BMW	38	

Brand	Rating	Notes
Lexus	38	
Scion	38	
Toyota	38	
Volvo	38	
Infiniti	37	
Nissan	37	
Acura	34	
Honda	34	
Jaguar	32	
Land Rover	32	
Mercedes-Benz	32	
Smart	32	
Porsche	28	
Volkswagen	28	
Kia	22	
Mitsubishi	-3	

Brand	Rating	Notes
Audi	-4	
Lamborghini	-4	
Subaru	-9	
Mazda	-20	

Fiat Chrysler Automobiles N.V.

Fiat Chrysler Automobiles N.V. (FCV) is a truly global company. It is an Italian-controlled company incorporated in the Netherlands, headquartered in London for tax purposes and listed on the New York Stock Exchange. While Fiat was founded in Italy in 1899 and Chrysler was founded in the United States in 1925, Fiat Chrysler was incorporated in 2014.

During the recession that began in 2007, Chrysler was guided through bankruptcy in a U.S. government bailout that led to a complete takeover by Fiat closing in 2014.

Brands owned by Fiat Chrysler include Fiat, Chrysler, Alpha Romeo, Dodge, Jeep, Maserati, RAM and several brands not sold in the United States. Over the past five years, American manufacturing jobs at Fiat Chrysler have been increasing.

Year Founded:	2014
Country:	The Netherlands
Global Employees:	238,162
U.S. Employees:	55,791 (23%)
Global Sales:	$123 billion
U.S. Sales:	$67.22 billion (55%)

Good for the USA Rating:

1) Headquarters:	The Netherlands	0 pts.
2) % U.S. employees (23) minus % U.S. sales (55) plus 50		18 pts.
3) 55,791 U.S. employees		46 pts.
4) U.S. Manufacturing:	YES	0 pts.
5) Foreign Manufacturing:	YES	0 pts.
Total Points		64 Points

General Motors Company

General Motors was guided through bankruptcy by the U.S. government, much like Chrysler; however, when GM emerged from bankruptcy in 2009, it closed several brands (Saturn, Hummer and Pontiac) and sold others, including Saab, before offering an IPO (initial public offering) for new shares in 2010.

Today, General Motors markets Chevrolet, GMC, Buick and Cadillac in the United States with additional brands throughout the world. Since the emergence from bankruptcy, American jobs at General Motors have been increasing.

Year Founded:	1908
Country:	United States
Global Employees:	216,000
U.S. Employees:	96,000 (44%)
Global Sales:	$152 billion
U.S. Sales:	$91 billion (60%)

Good for the USA Rating:

1) Headquarters:	USA	20 pts.
2) % U.S. employees (44) minus % U.S. sales (60) plus 50		34 pts.
3) 96,000 U.S. employees		86 pts.
4) U.S. Manufacturing:	YES	0 pts.
5) Foreign Manufacturing:	YES	0 pts.
Total Points		140 Points

Cars
(Alphabetical Order)

Brand	Rating	Notes
Acura	34	
Alfa Romeo	64	
Audi	-4	
BMW	38	
Buick	140	
Cadillac	140	
Chevrolet	140	
Chrysler	64	
Dodge	64	
Fiat	64	
Ford	88	
Genesis	45	
GMC	140	
Honda	34	
Hyundai	45	

Brand	Rating	Notes
Infiniti	37	
Jaguar	32	
Jeep	64	
Kia	22	
Lamborghini	-4	
Land Rover	32	
Lexus	38	
Lincoln	88	
Maserati	64	
Mazda	-20	
Mercedes-Benz	32	
MINI	39	
Mitsubishi	-3	
Nissan	37	
Porsche	28	
Ram	64	

Brand	Rating	Notes
Scion	38	
Smart	32	
Subaru	-9	
Toyota	38	
Tesla	122	
Volkswagen	28	
Volvo	38	

Computers & Accessories

This category ranges from 161 *Good for the USA* points at the top to -37 at the bottom. Some of the most popular brands are rated very low. Toshiba is the highest ranking foreign-owned brand and Magellan is the lowest rated at -37. This extremely low rating is because the parent company, Magellan, has only about 10% of their employees in the United States while they get fully 57% of their sales from American consumers.

As with all brands rated in *Good for the USA*, you should do your research, select two or three brands you would like to consider, and then see which brand gets the best rating. Then, share your purchase on social media and tell the world that *Good for the USA* tipped the choice to the brand you bought and away from your runners-up.

Following are the complete brand ratings from high to low and in alphabetical order. Between the high to low and alphabetical ratings, you'll find profiles of two companies.

Computers & Accessories
(Highest to Lowest Rating)

Brand	Rating	Notes
Amazon	161	
Intel	146	
Microsoft	125	
Apple	118	

Brand	Rating	Notes
HP	112	
Google	100	
Honeywell	85	
NETGEAR	70	
Kodak	64	
Nvidia	61	
GoPro	52	
Toshiba	48	
Lexmark	40	
Fujifilm	39	
Samsung	37	
Panasonic	34	
Garmin	26	
Lenovo	14	
Sharp	13	
Brother	6	

Brand	Rating	Notes
Canon	6	
Acer	1	
NEC	1	
Vaio	0	
Asus	-6	
D-Link	-7	
TomTom	-7	
HTC	-9	
Epson	-10	
Planar	-10	
AOC	-11	
Philips	-11	
LG	-15	
Nikon	-15	
RCA	-20	
Magellan	-37	

Honeywell

Honeywell was founded as the Honeywell Heating Specialty Company in Wabash, Indiana in 1906 by Mark Honeywell.

On December 31, 2015, Honeywell had 129,000 global employees with 49,000 (38%) in the United States. Ten years earlier, they had 116,000 global employees with 58,000 (43%) in the United States. The trend shows a global increase, but an American decrease.

Over that ten year period, Honeywell saw a 30% increase is U.S. sales (from $18 b to $23.8 b) with a 15% drop in American employees.

Year Founded: 1906
Country: United States
Global Employees: 129,000
U.S. Employees: 49,000 (38%)
Global Sales: $38.6 billion
U.S. Sales: $23.8 billion (62%)

Good for the USA Rating:

1) Headquarters: USA   20 pts.

2) % U.S. employees (38) minus % U.S. sales (62) plus 50   26 pts.

3) 49,000 U.S. employees   39 pts.

4) U.S. Manufacturing: YES   0 pts.

5) Foreign Manufacturing: YES   0 pts.

Total Points   85 Points

Lenovo Group Ltd.

Lenovo Group Ltd. was founded in Beijing, China in 1984 by ten engineers from a Chinese government group. In 2005, Lenovo purchased the IBM personal computer businesses from IBM including the ThinkPad laptop and tablet lines. In 2014, they purchased Motorola Mobility from Google. The purchase included smartphone lines Moto X, Moto G and Droid Turbo.

Rumors have claimed that Lenovo is a Chinese government owned company. The company has denied these rumors many times.

The U.S. employees are the result of the purchases of the IBM businesses, Motorola and other American-based companies. Lenovo says they have no plans to decrease American employment.

Year Founded:	1984
Country:	China
Global Employees:	60,000
U.S. Employees:	5,000 (8%)
Global Sales:	$45 billion
U.S. Sales:	$10.8 billion (24%)

Good for the USA Rating:

1) Headquarters:	China	0 pts.
2) % U.S. employees (8) minus % U.S. sales (24) plus 50		34 pts.
3) 5,000 U.S. employees		0 pts.
4) U.S. Manufacturing:	NO	-20 pts.
5) Foreign Manufacturing:	YES	0 pts.
Total Points		14 Points

Computers & Accessories
(Alphabetical Order)

Brand	Rating	Notes
Acer	1	
Apple	118	
Amazon	161	
AOC	-11	
Asus	-6	
Brother	6	
Canon	6	
D-Link	-7	
Epson	-10	
Fujifilm	39	
Garmin	26	
Google	100	
GoPro	52	
Honeywell	85	
HP	112	

Brand	Rating	Notes
HTC	-9	
Intel	146	
Kodak	64	
Lenovo	14	
Lexmark	40	
LG	-15	
Magellan	-37	
Microsoft	125	
NEC	1	
NETGEAR	70	
Nikon	-15	
Nvidia	61	
Panasonic	34	
Philips	-11	
Planar	-10	
RCA	-20	

Brand	Rating	Notes
Samsung	37	
Sharp	13	
TomTom	-7	
Toshiba	48	
Vaio	0	

Heating, Cooling & Air Quality Products

The highest rated brands in the Heating, Cooling and Air Quality category are Carrier and Bryant. They are both owned by United Technologies. The company's 120 *Good for the USA* points were earned because they employ about 65,000 Americans and have a nearly balanced chart of 33% U.S. employees and 38% U.S. sales. Carrier made national news during and after the 2016 Presidential election when they agreed to cancel a transfer of about 800 jobs to Mexico.

As with all brands rated in *Good for the USA*, you should do your research, select two or three brands you would like to consider, and then see which brand gets the best rating. Then, share your purchase on social media and tell the world that *Good for the USA* tipped the choice to the brand you bought and away from your runners-up.

Following are the complete brand ratings from high to low and in alphabetical order. Between the high to low and alphabetical ratings, you'll find profiles of two companies.

Heating, Cooling & Air Quality Products
(Highest to Lowest Rating)

Brand	Rating	Notes
Bryant	120	
Carrier	120	
3M	96	
Honeywell	85	

Brand	Rating	Notes
Keystone	70	
YORK	55	
Lennox	53	
DeWalt	48	
Hamilton Beach	48	
Amana	45	
Whirlpool	45	
Rheem	38	
Ruud	38	
Goodman	37	
Panasonic	34	
Electrolux	30	
Figidaire	30	
Friedrich	30	
Whynter	30	
Hoover	22	

Brand	Rating	Notes
Blueair	20	
American Standard	13	
Sharp	13	
Trane	9	
GE Appliance	5	
Haier	5	
LG	-15	

3M Company

Five businessmen founded 3M in 1902 as the Minnesota Mining and Manufacturing Company.

On December 31, 2015, 3M had 89,446 global employees with 35,973 (40%) in the United States. Ten years earlier, they had 69,315 global employees with 33,033 (48%) in the United States. The trend shows a strong global increase, but a minimal American increase.

Over that ten-year period, 3M saw a 45% increase is U.S. sales (from $8.3 b to $12.05 b), but only a 9% increase in American employees.

Year Founded:	1902
Country:	United States
Global Employees:	89,446
U.S. Employees:	35,973 (40%)
Global Sales:	$30.3 billion
U.S. Sales:	$12.05 billion (40%)

Good for the USA Rating:

1) Headquarters:	USA	20 pts.
2) % U.S. employees (40) minus % U.S. sales (40) plus 50		50 pts.
3) 35,973 U.S. employees		26 pts.
4) U.S. Manufacturing:	YES	0 pts.
5) Foreign Manufacturing:	YES	0 pts.
Total Points		96 Points

United Technologies

United Technologies was formed in 1975 when its name was changed from United Aircraft to reflect the new company's plan to diversify beyond aerospace.

On December 31, 2015, United Technologies had 197,200 global employees with 65,000 (33 %) in the United States. Ten years earlier, they had 222,200 global employees with 73,300 (33%) in the United States. The trend shows an equal decrease in domestic and foreign employment.

Over that ten-year period, United Technologies saw their American sales grow by less than one percent, while their foreign sales grew by nearly 25%.

Year Founded:	1975
Country:	United States
Global Employees:	197,200
U.S. Employees:	65,000 (33%)
Global Sales:	$56.5 billion
U.S. Sales:	$21.5 billion (38%)

Good for the USA Rating:

1) Headquarters:	USA	20 pts.
2) % U.S. employees (33) minus % U.S. sales (38) plus 50		45 pts.
3) 65,000 U.S. employees		55 pts.
4) U.S. Manufacturing:	YES	0 pts.
5) Foreign Manufacturing:	YES	0 pts.
Total Points		120 Points

Heating, Cooling & Air Quality Products
(Alphabetical Order)

Brand	Rating	Notes
3M	96	
Amana	45	
American Standard	13	
Blueair	20	
Bryant	120	
Carrier	120	
DeWalt	48	
Electrolux	30	
Friedrich	30	
Frigidaire	30	
GE Appliance	5	
Goodman	37	
Haier	5	
Hamilton Beach	48	
Honeywell	85	

Brand	Rating	Notes
Hoover	22	
Keystone	70	
Lennox	53	
LG	-15	
Panasonic	34	
Rheem	38	
Ruud	38	
Sharp	13	
Trane	9	
Whirlpool	45	
Whynter	30	
YORK	55	

Kitchen Appliances

The Kitchen Appliances category includes many American brands and foreign-owned brands in the 30 to 70 point range. The category also includes the only company we found that openly reports its sales and employees in the major countries they operate. Electrolux makes it very easy to learn that 17% of their employees are in the U.S. and they get 37% of their business from the United States. All other companies mask the facts about employee and sales locations.

As with all brands rated in *Good for the USA*, you should do your research, select two or three brands you would like to consider, and then see which brand gets the best rating. Then, share your purchase on social media and tell the world that *Good for the USA* tipped the choice to the brand you bought and away from your runners-up.

Following are the complete brand ratings from high to low and in alphabetical order. Between the high to low and alphabetical ratings, you'll find profiles of two companies.

Kitchen Appliances
(Highest to Lowest Rating)

Brand	Rating	Notes
Kenmore	200	
Sub-Zero	75	
Wolf	75	
Hitachi	56	

Brand	Rating	Notes
Hamilton Beach	48	
Viking	48	
Amana	45	
Jenn-Air	45	
KitchenAid	45	
Maytag	45	
Whirlpool	45	
Dacor	37	
Samsung	37	
Panasonic	34	
Electrolux	30	
Frigidaire	30	
Kucht	30	
Westinghouse	30	
Bosch	14	
Thermador	14	

Brand	Rating	Notes
Fisher & Paykel	5	
GE	5	
Haier	5	
Fagor	1	
ASKO	0	
Beko	0	
Blomberg	0	
Speed Queen	0	
Miele	-1	
Bertazzoni	-10	
Smeg	-10	
LG	-15	
RCA	-20	

Electrolux

Electrolux is a Swedish company. Globally, it is the second largest seller of appliances behind Whirlpool. Electrolux owns many brands including Electrolux, Frigidaire, Westinghouse and Eureka.

On December 31, 2015, Electrolux had 58,265 global employees with 9,701 (17%) in the United States. Ten years earlier, they had 69,523 global employees with 19,353 (28%) in the United States. The trend shows a global decrease, but an even greater decrease in U.S. employees.

Over that ten-year period, Electrolux saw their American sales increase five percent.

Year Founded:	1919
Country:	Sweden
Global Employees:	58,265
U.S. Employees:	9,701 (17%)
Global Sales:	$14.7 billion
U.S. Sales:	$5.5 billion (37%)

Good for the USA Rating:

1) Headquarters:	Sweden	0 pts.
2) % U.S. employees (17) minus % U.S. sales (37) plus 50		30 pts.
3) 9,701 U.S. employees		0 pts.
4) U.S. Manufacturing:	YES	0 pts.
5) Foreign Manufacturing:	YES	0 pts.
Total Points		30 Points

LG Electronics

LG Electronics was founded in 1958 in South Korea as Goldstar.

LG Electronics has a global workforce of about 77,000, but they have very few employees in the United States. They have announced plans to expand their workforce in the United States, with the stated possibility of a couple thousand American workers by 2020.

LG Electronics did not respond to our request for accurate American employee counts.

Year Founded:	1958
Country:	South Korea
Global Employees:	77,000
U.S. Employees:	320 (0%)
Global Sales:	$50.7 billion
U.S. Sales:	$12.7 billion (25%)

Good for the USA Rating:

1) Headquarters:	South Korea	0 pts.
2) % U.S. employees (0) minus % U.S. sales (25) plus 50		25 pts.
3) 320 U.S. employees		-20 pts.
4) U.S. Manufacturing:	NO	-20 pts.
5) Foreign Manufacturing:	YES	0 pts.
Total Points		-15 Points

Kitchen Appliances
(Alphabetical Order)

Brand	Rating	Notes
Amana	45	
ASKO	0	
Beko	0	
Bertazzoni	-10	
Blomberg	0	
Bosch	14	
Dacor	37	
Electrolux	30	
Fagor	1	
Fisher & Paykel	5	
GE	5	
Haier	5	
Hamilton Beach	48	
Hitachi	56	
Jenn-Air	45	

Brand	Rating	Notes
Kenmore	200	
KitchenAid	45	
Kucht	30	
LG	-15	
Maytag	45	
Miele	-1	
Panasonic	34	
RCA	-20	
Samsung	37	
Smeg	-10	
Sub-Zero	75	
Thermador	14	
Viking	48	
Westinghouse	30	
Whirlpool	45	
Wolf	75	

Laundry & Cleaning Products

Many of the same brands listed in the Kitchen Appliances category are also in this category. Some quick facts include; Maytag is owned by Whirlpool from the United States, Frigidaire is owned by Electrolux from Sweden and GE Appliances is not owned by GE, but by Haier Group from China.

As with all brands rated in *Good for the USA*, you should do your research, select two or three brands you would like to consider, and then see which brand gets the best rating. Then, share your purchase on social media and tell the world that *Good for the USA* tipped the choice to the brand you bought and away from your runners-up.

Following are the complete brand ratings from high to low and in alphabetical order. Between the high to low and alphabetical ratings, you'll find profiles of two companies.

Laundry & Cleaning products
(Highest to Lowest Rating)

Brand	Rating	Notes
Craftsman	224	
Kenmore	224	
Ridgid	75	
Black & Decker	48	
DeWalt	48	

Brand	Rating	Notes
Husqvarna	46	
Bissell	45	
Maytag	45	
Whirlpool	45	
Samsung	37	
Panasonic	34	
Electrolux	30	
Eureka	30	
Frigidaire	30	
Westinghouse	30	
Dirt Devil	23	
Hoover	23	
Oreck	23	
Royal	23	
Fisher & Paykel	5	
GE	5	

Brand	Rating	Notes
Speed Queen	0	
Miele	-1	
LG	-15	

Sears

Sears was founded in 1886 as Sears, Roebuck and Company by Richard Warren Sears and Alvah Curtis Roebuck. Sears was purchased by Kmart in 2005 and the combined company was named Sears Holding.

Sears owns brands including Kenmore Appliances and Craftsman tools. Kenmore Appliances are made for Sears by other companies like Electrolux and Whirlpool. Craftsman tools are mostly made in China.

Sears earns a very high *Good for the USA* rating even though their American employees don't make Kenmore or Craftsman products. The rating is earned because Sears employs 164,000 Americans. If you buy a Kenmore or Craftsman product, let Sears know you did it to support their American workers and you would prefer they move Craftsman manufacturing back to the United States.

Year Founded:	1886
Country:	United States
Global Employees	178,000
U.S. Employees:	164,000 (92%)
Global Sales:	$25 billion
U.S. Sales:	$23 billion (92%)

Good for the USA Rating:

1) Headquarters:	USA	20 pts.
2) % U.S. employees (92) minus % U.S. sales (92) plus 50		50 pts.
3) 164,000 U.S. employees		154 pts.
4) U.S. Manufacturing:	YES	0 pts.
5) Foreign Manufacturing:	YES	0 pts.
Total Points		224 Points

Techtronic Industries

Hoover, Dirt Devil, Oreck and Royal Vacuums . . . Ryobi, Milwaukee and Homelite Tools.

These sound like good, old American products, but they're not. They are all owned by a Chinese company.

Techtronic Industries was founded in Hong Kong in 1985. It bought Royal and Dirt Devil in 2003, Hoover in 2006, Oreck in 2013, Homelite and Ryobi in 2000, and Milwaukee in 2005.

The company still maintains a large American workforce. When you buy their products, let them know you want to see more American workers. They get seventy-six percent of their sales from American consumers.

Year Founded:	1985
Country:	China
Global Employees:	20,517
U.S. Employees:	10,000 (49%)
Global Sales:	$5 billion
U.S. Sales:	$3.8 billion (76%)

Good for the USA Rating:

1) Headquarters:	China	0 pts.
2) % U.S. employees (49) minus % U.S. sales (76) plus 50		23 pts.
3) 10,000 U.S. employees		0 pts.
4) U.S. Manufacturing:	YES	0 pts.
5) Foreign Manufacturing:	YES	0 pts.
Total Points		23 Points

Laundry & Cleaning products
(Alphabetical Order)

Brand	Rating	Notes
Bissell	45	
Black & Decker	48	
Craftsman	224	
DeWalt	48	
Dirt Devil	23	
Electrolux	30	
Eureka	30	
Fisher & Paykel	5	
Frigidaire	30	
GE	5	
Hoover	23	
Husqvarna	46	
Kenmore	224	
LG	-15	
Maytag	45	

Brand	Rating	Notes
Miele	-1	
Oreck	23	
Panasonic	34	
Ridgid	75	
Royal	23	
Samsung	37	
Speed Queen	0	
Westinghouse	30	
Whirlpool	45	

Motorcycles

Most motorcycles sold in the United States come from six countries around the world. On the *Good for the USA* list, only Harley-Davidson and Indian motorcycles are made in the USA; however, BMW, at 38 points, and Honda, at 34 points, still score well because they do have a lot of American workers in their auto businesses. After Honda, there is a substantial drop off to the other listed companies.

As with all brands rated in *Good for the USA*, you should do your research, select two or three brands you would like to consider, and then see which brand gets the best rating. Then, share your purchase on social media and tell the world that *Good for the USA* tipped the choice to the brand you bought and away from your runners-up.

Following are the complete brand ratings from high to low and in alphabetical order. Between the high to low and alphabetical ratings, you'll find profiles of two companies.

Motorcycles
(Highest to Lowest Rating)

Brand	Rating	Notes
Harley-Davidson	76	
Indian	53	
BMW	38	
Honda	34	

Brand	Rating	Notes
Aprilia	0	
Moto Guzzi	0	
Ducati	-4	
Kawasaki	-4	
Yamaha	-8	
Triumph	-10	

BMW Group

BMW was founded in 1916 in Munich, Bavaria, Germany as Bavarian Motor Works.

BMW began manufacturing motorcycles in 1917, followed by cars in 1928. Today, BMW owns the BMW brand, MINI and Rolls-Royce.

BMW opened its first American manufacturing facility in 1994 in South Carolina. The plant was originally expected to offer 2,000 jobs, but it has consistently employed about 8,000 Americans.

Year Founded: 1916
Country: Germany
Global Employees: 122,244
U.S. Employees: 9,000 (7%)
Global Sales: $103 billion
U.S. Sales: $19.4 billion (19%)

Good for the USA Rating:

1) Headquarters:	Germany	0 pts.
2) % U.S. employees (7) minus % U.S. sales (19) plus 50		38 pts.
3) 9,000 U.S. employees		0 pts.
4) U.S. Manufacturing:	YES	0 pts.
5) Foreign Manufacturing:	YES	0 pts.
Total Points		38 Points

Harley-Davidson Inc.

Harley-Davidson was founded in 1903 in Milwaukee, Wisconsin by William H. Harley, William A. Davidson and Walter Davidson, Jr. Today, Harley-Davidson has factories in Wisconsin, Pennsylvania, Missouri, Brazil and India.

Harley-Davidson is one of the few companies that have a higher percentage of employees (79%) in the United States than the percentage of their sales (73%) in the United States.

Year Founded:	1903
Country:	United States
Global Employees:	6,300
U.S. Employees:	5,000 (79%)
Global Sales:	$6 billion
U.S. Sales:	$4.4 billion (73%)

Good for the USA Rating:

1) Headquarters:	USA	20 pts.
2) % U.S. employees (79) minus % U.S. sales (73) plus 50		56 pts.
3) 5,000 U.S. employees		0 pts.
4) U.S. Manufacturing:	YES	0 pts.
5) Foreign Manufacturing:	YES	0 pts.
Total Points		76 Points

Motorcycles
(Alphabetical Order)

Brand	Rating	Notes
Aprilia	0	
BMW	38	
Ducati	-4	
Harley-Davidson	76	
Honda	34	
Indian	53	
Kawasaki	-4	
Moto Guzzi	0	
Triumph	-10	
Yamaha	-8	

Phones & Mobile Devices

Each year, it seems that more players get into the mobile phone business. At the top of the *Good for the USA* list you'll find six companies that all rate at or above 100 points. These are all very large American companies. They don't make their phones in the United States, but they do have hundreds of thousands of U.S. employees between them.

As with all brands rated in *Good for the USA*, you should do your research, select two or three brands you would like to consider, and then see which brand gets the best rating. Then, share your purchase on social media and tell the world that *Good for the USA* tipped the choice to the brand you bought and away from your runners-up.

Following are the complete brand ratings from high to low and in alphabetical order. Between the high to low and alphabetical ratings, you'll find profiles of two companies.

Phones & Mobile Devices
(Highest to Lowest Rating)

Brand	Rating	Notes
AT&T	210	
Amazon	161	
Microsoft	125	
Apple	118	
HP	112	

Brand	Rating	Notes
Nexus	100	
Barnes & Noble	68	
Hitachi	56	
DeWalt	48	
Fitbit	48	
Toshiba	48	
Sony	44	
Under Armor	44	
Samsung	37	
Garmin	26	
Kyocera	23	
Motorola	14	
Sharp	13	
BlackBerry	7	
BLU	5	
Bang & Olufsen	2	

Brand	Rating	Notes
OnePlus	0	
OPPO	0	
Vaio	0	
Asus	-6	
HTC	-9	
LG	-15	
VTech	-31	

Samsung Electronics

Samsung Electronics was established in 1969 in South Korea. Samsung has been the world's largest manufacturer of televisions since 2006 and the largest mobile phone maker since 2011.

With 319,000 global employees, Samsung has more employees than Apple (110,000), Google (62,000) and Microsoft (118,000) combined; however, Apple (60,000), Google (33,000) and Microsoft (60,000) each have more U.S.-based employees than Samsung (21,000).

Year Founded:	1969
Country:	South Korea
Global Employees:	319,000
U.S. Employees:	21,000 (7%)
Global Sales:	$180 billion
U.S. Sales:	$55.8 billion (31%)

Good for the USA Rating:

1) Headquarters:	South Korea	0 pts.
2) % U.S. employees (7) minus % U.S. sales (31) plus 50		26 pts.
3) 21,000 U.S. employees		11 pts.
4) U.S. Manufacturing:	YES	0 pts.
5) Foreign Manufacturing:	YES	0 pts.
Total Points		37 Points

Kyocera Corporation

Kyocera was founded in Japan in 1959 as Kyoto Ceramic Company, Limited. The name was changed to Kyocera Corporation in 1982 as it expanded well beyond ceramic products.

The Kyocera website claims it has about 3,000 U.S.-based employees and that they do some manufacturing in the United States. The twelve-point spread between their U.S.-based employees (4%) and U.S. sales (16%) helps their total *Good for the USA* score to stay above twenty.

Year Founded:	1959
Country:	Japan
Global Employees:	69,229
U.S. Employees:	3,000 (4%)
Global Sales:	$14.75 billion
U.S. Sales:	$2.4 billion (16%)

Good for the USA Rating:

1) Headquarters:	Japan	0 pts.
2) % U.S. employees (4) minus % U.S. sales (16) plus 50		38 pts.
3) 3,000 U.S. employees		-15 pts.
4) U.S. Manufacturing:	YES	0 pts.
5) Foreign Manufacturing:	YES	0 pts.
Total Points		23 Points

Phones & Mobile Devices
(Alphabetical Order)

Brand	Rating	Notes
Amazon	161	
Apple	118	
Asus	-6	
AT&T	210	
Bang & Olufsen	2	
Barnes & Noble	68	
BlackBerry	7	
BLU	5	
DeWalt	48	
Fitbit	48	
Garmin	26	
Hitachi	56	
HP	112	
HTC	-9	
Kyocera	23	

Brand	Rating	Notes
LG	-15	
Microsoft	125	
Motorola	14	
Nexus	100	
OnePlus	0	
OPPO	0	
Samsung	37	
Sharp	13	
Sony	44	
Toshiba	48	
Under Armor	44	
Vaio	0	
VTech	-31	

Tools & Power Equipment

This category has no companies rating above seventy-five points, and two companies come in as the lowest-rated brands on the *Good for the USA* list. WORX and Greenworks are two brands you'll see often in the big-box retailers. They're ratings are -47 and -51. Of course, it may be difficult to pass on the low prices of their products when you shop for tools.

As with all brands rated in *Good for the USA*, you should do your research, select two or three brands you would like to consider, and then see which brand gets the best rating. Then, share your purchase on social media and tell the world that *Good for the USA* tipped the choice to the brand you bought and away from your runners-up.

Following are the complete brand ratings from high to low and in alphabetical order. Between the high to low and alphabetical ratings, you'll find profiles of two companies.

Tools & Power Equipment
(Highest to Lowest Rating)

Brand	Rating	Notes
Ridgid	75	
Cub Cadet	65	
Remington	65	
Troy-Bilt	65	
Dremel	62	

Brand	Rating	Notes
Skil	62	
Black & Decker	47	
Bostitch	47	
Porter-Cable	47	
STANLEY	47	
Husqvarna	46	
Poulan	46	
OREGON	43	
LENOX	30	
Makita	27	
Homelite	22	
Milwaukee	22	
RYOBI	22	
ECHO	20	
Bosch	9	
Blue Max	0	

Brand	Rating	Notes
Rockwell	-47	
WORX	-47	
GreenWorks	-51	

Emerson Electric Company

Emerson was founded by John Wesley Emerson in 1890 in St. Louis, Missouri. Emerson became the first company to sell electric fans in the United States in 1892. As the availability of electricity expanded, Emerson offered electric sewing machines, dental drills and other power tools. Emerson owns the Ridgid brand of power tools and many other brands.

Year Founded:	1890
Country:	United States
Global Employees:	110,800
U.S. Employees:	31,000 (28%)
Global Sales:	$22.3 billion
U.S. Sales:	$9.8 billion (44%)

Good for the USA Rating:

1) Headquarters:	USA	20 pts.
2) % U.S. employees (28) minus % U.S. sales (44) plus 50		34 pts.
3) 31,000 U.S. employees		21 pts.
4) U.S. Manufacturing:	YES	0 pts.
5) Foreign Manufacturing:	YES	0 pts.
Total Points		75 Points

Stanley Black & Decker, Inc.

Stanley Works was founded in 1920 and Black & Decker was founded in 1910. The two companies merged in 2010 to form Stanley Black & Decker, Inc.

In May, 2002, Stanley considered moving its headquarters to Bermuda. Negative publicity convinced them to abandon the plan and they announced they would stay in the United Sates in August, 2002.

Year Founded:	2010
Country:	United States
Global Employees:	51,250
U.S. Employees:	13,533 (26%)
Global Sales:	$11.2 billion
U.S. Sales:	$5.9 billion (53%)

Good for the USA Rating:

1) Headquarters:	USA	20 pts.
2) % U.S. employees (26) minus % U.S. sales (53) plus 50		23 pts.
3) 13,533 U.S. employees		4 pts.
4) U.S. Manufacturing:	YES	0 pts.
5) Foreign Manufacturing:	YES	0 pts.
Total Points		47 Points

Tools & Power Equipment
(Alphabetical Order)

Brand	Rating	Notes
Black & Decker	47	
Blue Max	0	
Bosch	9	
Bostitch	47	
Cub Cadet	65	
Dremel	62	
ECHO	20	
GreenWorks	-51	
Homelite	22	
Husqvarna	46	
LENOX	30	
Makita	27	
Milwaukee	22	
OREGON	43	
Porter-Cable	47	

Brand	Rating	Notes
Poulan	46	
Remington	65	
Ridgid	75	
Rockwell	-47	
RYOBI	22	
Skil	62	
STANLEY	47	
Troy-Bilt	65	
WORX	-47	

CHAPTER SEVEN

PARENT COMPANY AND COUNTRY LIST

When shopping for a product, you should do your research and compare price and quality. Then, select two or three brands you would like to consider, and see which brand gets the best *Good for the USA* rating. Share your purchase on social media and tell the world that *Good for the USA* tipped the choice to the brand you bought and away from your runners-up. Please include #goodfortheUSA in your tweets and follow @GoodfortheUSA.

You should also consider directly letting the companies you considered know about your choice.

If enough people let companies and consumers know they purchased a brand—at least in part—because they employ Americans or didn't purchase a brand due to their lack of American employees, it might influence those companies to add to their employee roles in the United States. Best results will come from contacting the parent company. When Carrier was planning to move about 800 jobs to Mexico, then President-Elect Donald Trump convinced United Technologies, Carrier's parent company, to keep the jobs in the United States.

Following is the complete brand list in alphabetical order. After each brand, you'll see the parent company name, its home country and its *Good for the USA* rating.

Brand	Company	Country	Rating
3M	3M Company	USA	96
4moms	Thorley Industries LLC.	USA	40
A-Audio	A-Audio Headphones, Inc.	USA	30
Acer	Acer Group	Taiwan	1
Acura	Honda Motor Company, Ltd.	Japan	34
Advanced Fitness Group	Johnson Health Tech	Taiwan	-15
AKG	HARMAN International Industries	USA	67
Alfa Romeo	Fiat Chrysler Automobiles N.V.	Netherlands	64
Amana	Whirlpool Corporation	USA	45
Amazon	Amazon.com, Inc.	USA	161
American Girl	Mattel, Inc.	USA	2

Brand	Company	Country	Rating
American Standard	LIXIL Corporation	Japan	13
Anka	SCS Direct Inc.	USA	30
AOC	TPV Technology Limited	China	-11
AP Industries	AP Industries	Canada	0
Apple	Apple Inc.	USA	118
Aprica	Newell Rubbermaid	USA	30
Aprilia	Piaggio Group	Italy	0
ASKO	Gorenje Group	Slovenia	0
ASUS	ASUSTeK Computer Inc.	Taiwan	-6
AT&T	AT&T Inc.	USA	321
Attwood	Brunswick Corporation	USA	70
Audi	Audi AG	Germany	-4
Audio-Technica	Audio-Technica Corporation	Japan	-10
Audiovox	VOXX International Corporation	USA	-20
BabyBjörn	BabyBjörn AB	Sweden	-25
Baby Caché	Heritage Baby Products LLC	USA	30
Baby Einstein	Kids II	USA	38

Brand	Company	Country	Rating
Baby Mod	The MDB Family	USA	30
Babyletto	The MDB Family	USA	30
Baby's Dream	Baby's Dream Furniture, Inc.	USA	30
BÉABA	SCS Direct Inc.	USA	3
Bang & Olufsen	Bang & Olufsen Group	Denmark	2
Barnes & Noble	Barnes & Noble Booksellers, Inc.	USA	68
Bayliner	Brunswick Corporation	USA	70
Beats by Dre	Apple Inc.	USA	118
Beko	Arçelik A.Ş	Turkey	0
Bell Industries RPG	Brunswick Corporation	USA	70
Bertazzoni	BERTAZZONI SpA	Italy	-10
Bertram	Gavio Group	Italy	9
BH	BH S.A. Company	Spain	-10
Bissell	Bissell Homecare, Inc.	USA	45
Black & Decker	Stanley Black & Decker, Inc.	USA	47
BlackBerry	BlackBerry Limited	Canada	7
Blomberg	Arçelik A.Ş	Turkey	0
Bloom	Bloom Baby	USA	30

Brand	Company	Country	Rating
BLU	Blu Products	Brazil	5
Blueair	Unilever	UK	20
Blue Max	North American Tool Industries	USA	0
BMW	BMW Group	Germany	38
Bosch	BSH Hausgeräte GmbH	Germany	14
Bose	Bose Corporation	USA	70
Bostitch	Stanley Black & Decker, Inc.	USA	47
Boston Whaler	Brunswick Corporation	USA	70
Bright Starts	Kids II	USA	38
Brother	Brother Industries, Ltd	Japan	6
Bryant	United Technologies	USA	120
Buick	General Motors Company	USA	140
Cadillac	General Motors Company	USA	140
Cambridge Audio	Audio Partnership Plc	UK	-15
Cannondale	Dorel Industries	Canada	46
Canon	Canon Inc	Japan	6
Cariboo	SCS Direct Inc.	USA	30
Carrier	United Technologies	USA	120

Brand	Company	Country	Rating
Carter's	Carter's, Inc.	USA	54
Chaparral	Marine Products Corporation	USA	81
Chevrolet	General Motors Company	USA	140
Child of Mine	Carter's, Inc.	USA	54
Chrysler	Fiat Chrysler Automobiles N.V.	Netherlands	64
Clarion	Hitachi, Inc.	Japan	56
Coco	The Walt Disney Company	USA	195
Craftsman	Sears Holdings Co	USA	224
Crestliner	Brunswick Corporation	USA	70
Cub Cadet	MTD Holdings	USA	65
CYBEX	Goodbaby International Holdings	China	-7
Cybex	Brunswick Corporation	USA	70
Cypress Cay	Brunswick Corporation	USA	70
Dacor	Samsung Electronics	South Korea	37
DaVinci	The MDB Family	USA	30
Definitive Technology	DEI Holdings, Inc	USA	30
DeWalt	Stanley Black & Decker, Inc.	USA	47
Diamondback	Accell Group N.V.	Netherlands	25

Brand	Company	Country	Rating
Dirt Devil	Techtronic Industries Co. Ltd.	China	23
Disney	The Walt Disney Company	USA	95
Diversified Marine	Brunswick Corporation	USA	70
D-Link	D-Link Corp	Taiwan	-7
Dodge	Fiat Chrysler Automobiles N.V.	Netherlands	64
Dremel	Robert Bosch GmbH	Germany	62
Ducati	Audi AG	Germany	-4
ECHO	Yamabiko Corporation	Japan	20
Electrolux	Electrolux	Sweden	30
Epson	Seiko Epson Corporation	Japan	-10
Eureka	Electrolux	Sweden	30
Evenflo	Goodbaby International Holdings	China	-7
ExcerSaucer	Goodbaby International Holdings	China	-7
Fagor	Mondragon Corporation	Spain	1
Fiat	Fiat Chysler Automobiles N.V.	Netherlands	64
Figidaire	Electrolux	Sweden	30
Fisher & Paykel	Haier Group	China	5
Fisher-Price	Mattel, Inc.	USA	2

Brand	Company	Country	Rating
Fitbit	FitBit, Inc.	USA	48
Ford	Ford Motor Company	USA	88
Four Winns	The Beneteau Group	France	7
Friedrich	Friedrich Air Conditioning	USA	30
Frigidaire	Electrolux	Sweden	30
Fujifilm	Fujifilm Holdings Corporation	Japan	39
Garmin	Garmin Ltd.	Switzerland	26
GE Appliance	Haier Group	China	5
Genesis	Hyundai Motor Company	South Korea	45
Genuine Kids	Carter's, Inc.	USA	54
GMC	General Motors Company	USA	140
GoPro	GoPro, Inc.	USA	52
Goodman	Daikin Group	Japan	37
Google	Alphabet Inc.	USA	100
Graco	Newell Rubbermaid	USA	30
Grady-White	Grady-White Boats, Inc.	USA	70
GreenWorks	Changzhou Globe Tools Co. Ltd.	China	-51
Haier	Haier Group	China	5

Brand	Company	Country	Rating
Hamilton Beach	NACCO Industries, Inc	USA	48
Hammer Strength	Brunswick Corporation	USA	70
Harley-Davidson	Harley-Davidson, Inc	USA	76
Harman Kardon	Harman International Industries	USA	67
Harris	Brunswick Corporation	USA	70
Hitachi	Hitachi, Inc.	Japan	56
Homelite	Techtronic Industries Co. Ltd.	China	23
Honda	Honda Motor Company, Ltd.	Japan	34
Honeywell	Honeywell International, Inc.	USA	85
Hoover	Techtronic Industries Co. Ltd.	China	23
Horizon Fitness	Johnson Health Tech	Taiwan	-15
HP	HP Inc.	USA	112
HTC	HTC Company	Taiwan	-9
Husqvarna	Husqvarna AB	Sweden	46
Hyundai	Hyundai Motor Company	South Korea	45
Indian	Polaris Industries, Inc	USA	53
Infiniti	Nissan Motor Company Ltd	Japan	37
InMovement	Brunswick Corporation	USA	70

Brand	Company	Country	Rating
Insignia	Best Buy Co. Inc.	USA	161
InStep	The Walt Disney Company	USA	195
Intel	Intel Corporation	USA	146
ION Audio	BH S.A. company	Spain	-10
Jaguar	Tata Group	India	32
JBL	Harman International Industries	USA	67
Jeep	Fiat Chysler Automobiles N.V.	Netherlands	64
Jenn-Air	Whirlpool Corporation	USA	45
Just One You	Carter's, Inc.	USA	54
JVC	JVCKenwood Group	Japan	-19
Kawasaki	Kawasaki Heavy Industries, Ltd.	Japan	-4
Kellogg Marine	Brunswick Corporation	USA	70
Kenmore	Sears Holdings Co	USA	224
Kenwood	JVCKenwood Group	Japan	-19
Kettler	Kettler	Germany	-20
Keystone	Keystone Manufacturing Co.	USA	70
Kia	Kia Motors Corp.	South Korea	22
KitchenAid	Whirlpool Corporation	USA	45

Brand	Company	Country	Rating
Kitvision	Kondor Ltd.	UK	-20
Klipsch	VOXX International Corporation	USA	-20
Kodak	Eastman Kodak	USA	64
Kolcraft	Kolcraft Enterprises Inc	USA	30
Koss	Koss Corporation	USA	50
KTM	Cross Industries AG	Austria	-10
Kucht	Kucht	USA	30
Kyocera	Kyocera Corporation	Japan	23
Lamborghini	Audi AG	Germany	-4
Land 'N' Sea	Brunswick Corporation	USA	70
Land Rover	Tata Group	India	32
Lanier	Ricoh Company, Ltd	Japan	41
Lennox	Lennox International Inc.	USA	53
Lenovo	Lenovo	China	14
LENOX	Newell Rubbermaid	USA	30
Lexmark	Lexmark International Inc.	USA	40
Lexus	Toyota Motor Corporation	Japan	38
LG	LG Electronics Inc.	South Korea	-15

Brand	Company	Country	Rating
Life Fitness	Brunswick Corporation	USA	70
LÍLLÉbaby	SCS Direct, Inc.	USA	30
Lincoln	Ford Motor Company	USA	88
LiveStrong	Johnson Health Tech	Taiwan	-15
Lowe Boats	Brunswick Corporation	USA	70
Lund	Brunswick Corporation	USA	70
Magellan	MiTAC Holdings Corporation	Taiwan	-37
Magnavox	Koninklijke Philips N.V.	Netherlands	54
Makita	Makita	Japan	27
Malibu Boats	Malibu Boats, Inc.	USA	47
Mariner	Brunswick Corporation	USA	70
Maserati	Fiat Chysler Automobiles N.V.	Netherlands	64
MasterCraft	MCBC Holdings Inc.	USA	80
Maxi-Cosi	Dorel Industries	Canada	46
Maytag	Whirlpool Corporation	USA	45
Mazda	Mazda Motor Corporation	Japan	-20
Mercedes-Benz	Daimler AG	Germany	32
Mercury	Brunswick Corporation	USA	70

Brand	Company	Country	Rating
Meridian Yachts	Brunswick Corporation	USA	70
Micralite	SCS Direct, Inc.	USA	30
Microsoft	Microsoft Corporation	USA	125
Miele	Miele	Germany	-1
Milwaukee	Techtronic Industries Co. Ltd.	China	23
MINI	BMW Group	Germany	38
Mitsubishi	Mitsubishi Motors Corporation	Japan	-3
Mongoose	Dorel Industries	Canada	46
Moto Guzzi	Piaggio & C. SpA	Italy	0
MotorGuide	Brunswick Corporation	USA	70
Motorola	Lenovo	China	14
NEC	NEC Corp.	Japan	1
NETGEAR	Netgear, Inc.	USA	70
Nexus	Google	USA	100
Nikon	Nikon Corporation	Japan	-15
Nintendo	Nintendo Co., Ltd	Japan	13
Nissan	Nissan Motor Company Ltd	Japan	37
NordicTrack	ICON Health & Fitness	USA	85

Brand	Company	Country	Rating
Nursery Works	The MDB Family	USA	30
Nvidia	Nvidia Corporation	USA	61
Olympus	Olympus	Japan	16
OnePlus	BBK Electronics Corp Ltd.	China	0
OPPO	BBK Electronics	China	0
Oreck	Techtronic Industries Co. Ltd.	China	23
OREGON	Blount International	USA	43
OshKosh B'gosh	Carter's, Inc.	USA	54
Panasonic	Panasonic Corporation	Japan	34
Parrot	Parrot SA	France	-11
Pentax	Ricoh Company, Ltd	Japan	41
Phiaton	Cresyn Co., Ltd	South Korea	-19
Philips	TPV Technology, LTD	China	-11
Planar	Leyard Optoelectronic Co., Ltd.	China	-10
Polk Audio	DEI Holdings, Inc	USA	30
Porsche	Volkswagen Group	Germany	28
Porter-Cable	Stanley Black & Decker, Inc.	USA	47
Pottery Barn Kids	Williams-Sonoma, Inc.	USA	84

Brand	Company	Country	Rating
Poulan	Husqvarna AB	Sweden	46
Precious Firsts	Carter's, Inc.	USA	54
Princecraft	Brunswick Corporation	USA	70
ProForm	ICON Health & Fitness	USA	85
PSB	The Lenbrook Group	Canada	0
Quicksilver	Brunswick Corporation	USA	70
Quinny	Dorel Industries	Canada	46
Raleigh	Accell Group N.V.	Netherlands	25
Ram	Fiat Chysler Automobiles N.V.	Netherlands	64
RCA	VOXX International Corporation	USA	-20
Regal	Regal Marine Industries, Inc	USA	90
Remington	MTD Holdings	USA	65
Rheem	Paloma Co., Ltd.	Japan	38
Ricoh	Ricoh Company, Ltd	Japan	41
Ridgid	Emerson Electric Company	USA	75
Robalo	Marine Products Corporation	USA	81
Rockwell	Positec Tool Corporation	China	-47
Rollplay	Goodbaby International Holdings	China	-7

Brand	Company	Country	Rating
Royal	Techtronic Industries Co. Ltd.	China	23
Ruud	Paloma Co., Ltd.	Japan	38
RYOBI	Techtronic Industries Co. Ltd.	China	23
Safety 1st	Dorel Industries	Canada	46
Samsung	Samsung Electronics	South Korea	37
Savin	Ricoh Company, Ltd	Japan	41
Sceptre	Sceptre, Inc.	USA	20
Schwinn	Dorel Industries	Canada	46
Scion	Toyota Motor Corporation	Japan	38
Sea Ray	Brunswick Corporation	USA	70
Sennheiser	Sennheiser Electronic	Germany	25
Sharp	Sharp Corporation	Japan	13
Skil	Robert Bosch GmbH	Germany	62
Smart	Daimler AG	Germany	32
SmartCraft	Brunswick Corporation	USA	70
Smeg	BERTAZZONI SpA	Italy	-10
Sony	Sony Corporation	Japan	44
Speed Queen	BDT Capital Partners	Canada	0

Brand	Company	Country	Rating
STANLEY	Stanley Black & Decker, Inc.	USA	47
Star Cruisers	Yamaha Motor Corporation	Japan	-8
Subaru	Fuji Heavy Industries, Ltd	Japan	-9
Sub-Zero	Sub-Zero Group, Inc.	USA	75
Suzuki	Suzuki Motor Corporation	Japan	8
SVAN	SCS Direct Inc.	USA	30
Swivl-Eze	Brunswick Corporation	USA	70
TCL	TCL Corporation	China	-11
Tesla	Tesla Motors, Inc.	USA	122
Thermador	BSH Hausgeräte GmbH	Germany	14
Thunder Jet	Brunswick Corporation	USA	70
Tivoli Audio	Tivoli Audio Inc.	USA	30
TomTom	TomTom International BV	Netherlands	-7
Toshiba	Toshiba Corp	Japan	48
Toyota	Toyota Motor Corporation	Japan	38
Trane	Ingersoll Rand	Ireland	9
Triumph	Triumph Motorcycles Ltd	UK	-10
Troy-Bilt	MTD Holdings	USA	65

Brand	Company	Country	Rating
Under Armour	Under Armour, Inc.	USA	44
Urbini	Goodbaby International Holdings	China	-7
Vaio	BBK Electronics	China	0
Viking	Middleby Corporation	USA	48
Vision	Johnson Health Tech	Taiwan	-15
Vizio	LeEco	China	2
Volkswagen	Volkswagen Group	Germany	28
Volvo	The Volvo Group	Sweden	38
VTech	Vtech Holdings Ltd.	China	-31
Wellcraft	The Beneteau Group	France	7
Westinghouse	Electrolux	Sweden	30
Whale	Brunswick Corporation	USA	70
Whirlpool	Whirlpool Corporation	USA	45
Whynter	Whynter LLC.	USA	30
Withings	Nokia Corporation	Finland	31
Wolf	Sub-Zero Group, Inc.	USA	75
WORX	Positec Tool Corporation	China	-47
Yamaha	Yamaha Motor Corporation	Japan	-8

Brand	Company	Country	Rating
Yamaha Boats	Yamaha Motor Corporation	Japan	-8
YORK	Johnson Controls Intl. PLC	Ireland	55
ZVOX	ZVOX Audio, LLC	USA	30

CHAPTER EIGHT

THE *GOOD FOR THE USA* RATING SYSTEM

Following is a closer look at the rating system to explain how the rating can show what's *Good for the USA*.

1. **U.S. Headquarters   20 point**s

   If a company is incorporated in the United States, it is, at least, in a position to pay U.S. corporate taxes. Foreign companies often avoid these taxes. For this reason, we award U.S.-based companies twenty points and foreign-based companies no points.

   Of course, just because a company is based in the United States, it doesn't mean that company is contributing to the economy of the United States. It could import all of its products from overseas and employ few U.S. workers.

   That's why the *Good for the USA* rating system goes

beyond the "buy from an American company" theory.

2. **Percentage of total employees based in the United States minus the percentage of total sales generated in the United States plus an additional 50 points.**

The ideal company would have an equal percentage of U.S. employees to sales in the United States. If a company generates half of its global sales in the United States, it should have half of its employees in the United States. If that same "ideal" company generated the other half of its sales in Europe, it should have half its employees in Europe. Such a company would be a true global company. It would contribute as much to each nation's economy as it gets back in sales. This category is best explained by an example.

Honda has 208,399 employees worldwide. It employs 29,500 people in the United States. That means 14% of all Honda employees work in the United States.

Honda had total sales of $144 billion in 2015. Approximately 50% of those sales were made in the United States. That means fully half of Honda's global sales in 2015 came from the United States.

And what does the U.S. economy get for all that money transferring to Japan? We get 29,500 American jobs, or 14% of Honda's total employment.

In the *Good for the USA* rating, Honda gets 14 points minus 50 points plus 50 points equaling 14 total points for category two. The 50 points are added to every company's total so that most companies will yield a positive rating.

Compare General Motors to Honda and we see that GM has 44% of their employees in the United States (96,000 of 216,000 total employees). GM generates 60% of their sales in the United States, yielding 34 points in category two . . . 44 minus 60 plus 50.

Category two only rates the ratio of employees to sales; therefore, a company with even a very small number of employees could yield a higher score in category two than General Motors.

For example, Tesla Motors has about 13,058 global employees with 12,878 in the United States. Tesla generates half of its sales in the United States, so their rating is 99 points (99% U.S. employees minus 50% U.S. sales plus 50). It's clear that General Motor's 96,000 U.S. employees contribute more to our national economy than Tesla's 12,878 employees.

That's why category three is included in the *Good for the USA* rating system.

3. Bonus Points for Total Amount of U.S. Employees.

In the example for category two, Honda has 29,500 U.S. employees and General Motors has 96,000.

General Motors earned 34 points compared to Honda's 14 points due to GM's stronger jobs to revenue ratio (44% U.S. employees versus 60% U.S. sales). Obviously, GM's 96,000 employees contribute more to the U.S. economy than Honda's 29,500 employees.

Category three picks up where category two left off. Here, the *Good for the USA* rating system awards points for total amount of U.S. employees. Points are awarded as follows:

Zero to 1,000 U.S. employees earns minus (-) 20 points

1,001 to 5,000 U.S. employees earns minus (-) 15 points

5,001 to 10,000 U.S. employees earns zero points

More than 10,000 U.S. employees earns one point for every 1,000 employees over 10,000.

General Motors earns 86 additional points for its 96,000 U.S. employees. Honda earns 20 additional points for its 29,500 U.S. employees. And Tesla earns an additional 3 points for its 12,878 U.S. employees.

This is where the rating system allows the companies with the most U.S. employees to rise above the rest.

In many sections, foreign companies outscore American-based companies because they employ a lot of Americans.

After all, Americans need jobs and the companies that supply those jobs deserve our business.

4. **No U.S. Manufacturing   -20 points**

Some companies, both domestic and foreign, have only management personnel in the United States. If they don't manufacture any of their products in the United States, the company will lose twenty points.

5. **No Foreign Manufacturing   +20 points**

Not many companies earn these points. In fact, very few U.S. companies have a larger percentage of U.S. employees than sales. Compare this to many foreign companies and you'll find Japan, Germany and several other developed countries still have many large companies that have a greater percentage of domestic employees than sales. Often, this is because they are exporting their products to the United States. Your dollars are then used to pay workers in their home country and help their economies grow.

Staying in the automotive category, an example of this is Mazda. The Japanese car manufacturer maintains 76% of its workers in Japan but only generates 15% of its sales from Japan.

Thirty (30) percent of Mazda sales are from the United States. With only a few U.S. employees and no U.S. manufacturing, Mazda is good for Japan's economy, but not Good for the USA. Mazda earns a *Good for the USA* rating of -20. If this was a *Good for Japan* book, Mazda would earn a rating of 165.

No U.S.-based car company earns a rating that high. In fact, no American company comes close to the 76% of employees and 15% of sales ratio that Mazda has in Japan. High ratios like Mazda's are frequent in most other countries, but not in the United States.

There you have it. The *Good for the USA* rating system—it rewards companies that show an interest in keeping or adding employees in the United States and uncovers companies that care only about the bottom line. To use this book when you shop for new items, simply turn to the section that lists ratings for the type of product you plan to buy. The first page in each section lists the brands in order from highest rating to lowest. Next, is an alphabetical list of the brands and their ratings. Between these lists is a profile of two companies showing where they earned or lost points. Comments regarding the listed company can be found at the top of some of the pages. For example, Electrolux, a Swedish company, is highlighted as the company that is the most forthcoming about global employment and sales figures. They list employment and sales by country on their website.

Most companies refuse to release United States employee counts. They list total global employees and, occasionally, regional employee totals, but rarely U.S. employees. The newest method of hiding U.S. job losses is to list North American employees and North American sales. While we have nothing against Canada and Mexico, it seems disingenuous to combine them with the United States to report employees and sales. Our research has shown that for most companies, the United States represents between 85% and 95% of their North American sales.

Every effort was made to be as accurate as possible. Our research always begins with the annual report of publicly traded companies. Writing to companies or calling to ask for the information proved unsuccessful. Most simply ignored our request or said the U.S. government doesn't require them to make that information public. The U.S. government does require all companies with more than 100 employees to file an Equal Employment Opportunity report to monitor diversity trends in hiring. That report lists the total number of employees in the U.S.

at each company, but the government does not release the data. Some companies make the report public, but most do not.

Next, we searched each company's websites followed by government records and news reports. Prior to publication we contacted each company with the numbers we planned to use in the book. They were all given the opportunity to update the numbers. No companies chose to participate. It almost seems as if they have something to hide. Could it be they don't want the consumers in the largest market in the world to know where the jobs are?

It was also surprisingly difficult to determine sales figures for the United States. Many companies have switched to releasing sales data by region. The United States falls into the North America region along with Canada and Mexico. While the United States supplies the overwhelming majority of sales in the North America region, jobs often are found in Mexico. This allows the companies to release more balanced figures for jobs versus sales without saying the jobs are in Mexico and the sales are in the USA. To find the actual numbers, we compared several corporate documents to reveal more accurate figures for the United States alone.

We are confident that our final ratings are accurate relative to each company in each category. It is hoped that as this book becomes more popular, companies will be more willing to release United States-specific information.

You might be wondering how using this book will work when so many "Buy American" campaigns have failed. "Buy American" does nothing to influence foreign companies to hire American employees. If nobody bought Honda cars because they aren't an American company, 29,500 Americans would be out of work. This book seeks to influence Honda to hire more Americans and make more of their cars in the United States. If you decide to buy a Honda car, write them a letter, send them an email or post to social media sites and tell them you bought a Honda, in part, because they employ 29,500 Americans. If you choose to purchase a General Motors car, contact Honda and tell them you didn't buy a Honda because they only have 14% of their employees in the United States compared to 50% of their sales. To make this letter writing and social media posting easier, you'll find a full list of the brands, their parent companies and their home country in Chapter Seven. Post about the brands, but write to and digitally contact the parent companies.

ABOUT THE AUTHOR

Thomas Johnson is founder and President of Zuchelli & Johnson Advertising, Inc. He has more than thirty years of experience creating and managing marketing projects for domestic and foreign companies of all sizes. He has personally seen the impact on people and communities as manufacturing jobs leave the United States. He has also seen many foreign-based companies become job producers in the United States. He wrote *Good for the USA Buyer's Guide* with the hope that both domestic and foreign companies will try to be better supporters of American workers. A strong and growing economy in the United States is good for Americans, companies, and indeed, for all the people in the world.

www.ingramcontent.com/pod-product-compliance
Lightning Source LLC
Chambersburg PA
CBHW062146280526
45788CB00001B/331